Alfred Deller is more than a sing[er] [...]
musical experience. As with m[...]
experiences, it is at first hearing somewhat
of a shock when, from his great frame and
masculine presence, there issue high,
flute-like sounds, ranging the register of
the female alto, yet unmistakably male in
character.

Until the advent of Deller the art of the
countertenor—a male alto of exceptional
range and flexibility—had been lost since
the seventeenth century, driven into
obscurity by the popularity of the Italian
castrati. Because of this, a vast quantity of
Elizabethan music, and that of Purcell,
who was also a countertenor, has to this
day been completely neglected, and it has
been Alfred Deller's good fortune to be
able to introduce it to modern audiences,
for whom it has proved a refreshing
contrast to nineteenth-century
romanticism and twentieth-century
serialism.

Alfred Deller has himself a touch of the
Elizabethan : a blend of artistic sensibility,
religious preoccupation, infectious gaiety
and brooding melancholy, which is
admirably brought out in this absorbing
biography. But it is difficult to see where
he gets it from, for he comes of solid,
working-class stock, his father an Army
P.T. instructor who disciplined his
children as he had done the soldiers under
his charge. Amazingly, Alfred, possessed

STOUR MUSIC
1963

OLANTIGH

by permission of F. W. H. Loudon, Esq., and Lady Prudence Loudon

A concert of

ENGLISH MUSIC OF THE

SIXTEENTH AND SEVENTEENTH CENTURY

PROGRAMME

Saturday, 29th June, 7.30 p.m.

Price 1/-

ALFRED DELLER

A Singularity of Voice

by

MICHAEL AND MOLLIE HARDWICK

with a Foreword by Sir Michael Tippett

Illustrated by John Ward, R.A.

CASSELL · LONDON

Other books by Michael & Mollie Hardwick include:

THE CHARLES DICKENS COMPANION

THE SHERLOCK HOLMES COMPANION

THE MAN WHO WAS SHERLOCK HOLMES

(all published by John Murray)

WRITERS' HOUSES: A LITERARY JOURNEY IN ENGLAND

(Phoenix House)

CASSELL & COMPANY LTD
35 Red Lion Square, London WC1
Melbourne, Sydney, Toronto
Johannesburg, Auckland

© Michael and Mollie Hardwick 1968
First published 1968

S.B.N. 304 91694 3

Printed in Great Britain by
The Camelot Press Ltd., London and Southampton
F. 168

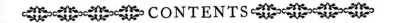 CONTENTS

ACKNOWLEDGEMENTS

The authors acknowledge with gratitude the help of many people, including: Dr Walter Bergmann, Canon L. John Collins, Mr Desmond Dupré, the Revd. and Mrs Geoffrey Keable, Professor Anthony Lewis, Mr Cyril Macartney, Mrs Ruth I. MacLaughlin, Canon Joseph Poole, Sir Michael Tippett, Sir Jack Westrup, members of the Deller Consort, members of the Deller family, the Principals and staffs of the Royal Academy of Music and the Royal College of Music, the Librarian and staff of the Central Music Library, Westminster Public Libraries; and Mrs Margaret Morton, for invaluable secretarial assistance.

We are grateful to Mr Benjamin Britten and Mr Peter Pears for permission to quote letters.

FOREWORD
by Sir Michael Tippett

This book tells a fascinating story, stretching as it does from a childhood which might almost be described as hang-over Dickensian (the authors even mention Gradgrind, though Dickens died forty-two years before Alfred Deller was born) to an international music career in the permissive society of the present time. Part of the fascination is the clear fact that Deller doesn't quite fit into either. He certainly hasn't ruled his family as his father ruled his mother and his siblings. But aspects of our present society disturb him deeply, if we are to judge by his fulmination against beat groups. This all comes somehow, I think, from the integral quality of his Christianity. Gladys Keable speaks of this in the book: 'In bringing out the whole beauty of music he is bringing out something that is a beautiful part of life, and of the Trinity.' I can echo the first part of that sentence, but not the end; so that I have to make a special effort to imagine that if one felt the beauty of music in such terms then one might really feel 'convinced (with respect to beat music) that the whole question of dope-taking and juvenile delinquency is all linked up with this rotten influence'. This is surely the tremendous tradition of the arts as moral or immoral influences, which runs from Plato to the Puritans. It is hard to live by it nowadays.

The book is not merely a success story. Deller has suffered more than most great artists from the negative sides of his genius: professional self-depreciation and insecurity; emotional depression. It is up to professional colleagues to help an artist with the former, as it is the burden of wife or friend to deal with the latter (Peggy Deller fully understands this). But Deller has had to face extra problems and overcome peculiar susceptibilities owing to the very nature of his voice. And again it is ironical to note that present-day young people, hearing a lot of beat where voices are high or low quite irrespective of sex, and generally accepting our permissive society where virility is no longer a he-man mythology, must find Deller's worries about his voice, as he talks of them in this book, outside their ken.

Yet it is a success story; not only of a great singer, but of music itself—especially English music. For Deller is of the generation where Purcell and the Elizabethans have truly returned to find their public. Our musical forefathers worked hard to bring this about, as we have worked hard. But the moment was not ripe for them, while we have seen the flowering. It was always known to history books that *Music for a while* was in its way as fine as Dido's Lament. But the public only knew this, or was even willing to know this, through Deller's first recording. In the same way it is Deller's generation that first carried English music abroad, to an at last relatively unprejudiced foreign public. To Germany, Purcell, and to a lesser degree the Elizabethans, was as much a revelation as, say, Monteverdi was to us. It was also the same in America. For just because we accept as automatic that the roots of American literature are English, we find it sometimes difficult to realize that the roots of American concert music are German. (Jazz is, of course, not German at all: but Deller does not belong to that story.) So that until the prejudice and falsity of the older notions of the non-musicality of our country gave over, there was little to be done. Now, it is safe to say, that has all changed and Deller is one of England's most successful artists over the whole of that vast land.

I have stressed the more impersonal aspects of Deller's success story because this is where his true immortality must rest. Not so much because such an artist issued from such an apparently unpropitious family, or that he had to wait so many years to find his own means to maturity and fulfilment, but because he is a particular and special musician among the select group of internationally esteemed performers, and in his field unique.

INTRODUCTION

Alfred Deller is more than a singer: he is a musical experience. As with many new experiences, there is some shock attending a first hearing of him, when, from that great frame and manly presence, there issue those high, flute-like sounds, ranging the register of the female alto, yet unmistakably masculine in character. He recognizes this reaction as something which he has to accept: 'I have trained myself not to be upset by it,' he says, 'and I only hope that the audience will quickly get over this natural surprise and settle down to listen to the voice as a musical instrument. Thank heaven, most people do.'

What they hear then is something unique, not in the sense of freak, but a consummate artistry and emotional instinct, expressed in a long-lost voice type intimately associated with the golden age of English music of the sixteenth and seventeenth centuries, driven into obscurity with that music by eighteenth-century Italianism and nineteenth-century romanticism, and resurrected unwittingly by the self-taught Deller in our own time. It is as though an amateur archaeologist had stumbled upon a treasure of infinite value, and had possessed the gifts and instinctive resources to make himself the world's leading expert on it.

Therefore, listening to Deller is to tune in directly to those golden times of Dowland, Campion and then Purcell, whose perfection is instantly recognizable and is especially acceptable to a younger generation who do not care to wallow in sticky romanticism but find the engineered music of our time unable to fulfil that emotional function which is music's chief *raison d'être*. The music in which Deller mainly deals proves to be of timeless vitality, and, especially in the case of Dowland, surprisingly modern idiom. It is the kind of antique which one chooses to live with, rather than relegate to the cabinet.

Believers in reincarnation would have little difficulty in making out a case based on Deller himself. There is more of the Tudor to him than that beard: an un-modern blend of artistic sensibility, religious preoccupation, infectious gaiety and brooding melancholy. 'In that moment, the centuries rolled back,' Michael Tippett recalls of first hearing Deller sing: merely to meet him is to experience something of the same sort.

A great part of the fascination of Deller's story is to watch it taking shape, from the most inauspicious of beginnings, moving from phase to phase with a smooth precision which most of us must envy. Again and again, we see the cue given and perfectly taken; the apparently chance circumstance producing a significant outcome; the seemingly unremarkable encounter leading to a relationship of major importance in his life or art. There is something decidedly mystical about it: from the beginning, Deller has had no doubt about the nature of the mystery.

Uniquely gifted, he has been led by his art along a path lonelier than he might have chosen to tread. World-wide renown has, ironically, brought him few of the comforts of life, in that the home pleasures he values have had to be sacrificed increasingly to the demands of the travelling he dislikes. Peggy, the wife and helpmeet to whom he owes so much, now sees less of him than when he was unknown. Paradoxically, the country whose greatest music he has helped to achieve universal respect sees least of him. For two-thirds of every year he is abroad, singing to packed and ever-appreciative audiences throughout America and Europe, and in the Antipodes and the East. It is one of his regrets that England paid less heed to him when it might have done, so that now, when invited to perform here, he has often to refuse because of an overseas commitment. He has received no public or academic honour in this country, for all his work's influence upon the foreign view of our artistic capacity: but he is not alone in this.

In the final analysis, such things matter little to Alfred Deller. Though he may regret that which he does not have, or had and has lost, he is conscious above all of standing in the very centre of his true circle, a man born and destined to do what he is doing, and humbly aware of the God-given privilege this represents. Gladys Keable has said that everything he does is an act of worship: he would be the last to deny it, or to presume to question his rôle.

For nature doth more commonly bestow such a singularitie of voice upon boyes and striplings, than upon men.

THOMAS CORYATE (1577–1617)

The name once meant 'Dweller in the dell'. Robert atte Delle lived in Sussex in 1296, and there were families elsewhere named Dellere, Dellar, Delleman and Dell. There may be Flemish associations and some connection with Huguenot settlers in this country.

For one whose character and art and even appearance might seem to be in the nature of a throwback to the late Middle Ages, Alfred Deller is surprisingly unconcerned about his origins. He did not know his grandparents on either side, and has never been much moved to enquire about them. All he does know is that his father's family lived in Hertfordshire and is not related to the only other sizeable Deller clan in England still, whose cafés have been refreshing West Country folk for many years.

His father, Thomas William Deller, was born in Ware, Hertfordshire, on 7 February 1872, the son of a doctor's coachman who contracted smallpox from one of his employer's patients and died of it, aged twenty-one. He left a widow, who married again twice, a daughter, and the one son, William, who left school at twelve and went to work on the land. In those days of Hiring Fairs, at which agricultural employers took on their labour for the coming year, a familiar sight was a resplendent recruiting sergeant, seated with his drummer outside an inn and, with beer and eloquence, cajoling young men into accepting the Queen's Shilling. One of these martial evangelists so moved young William Deller's spirit that he offered to testify in the appropriate way. The sergeant laughed and told him to stay on the land and grow up a little before trying again.

When he was fourteen, armed with a recommendation of character, he left the village for London, where he stayed with an uncle and aunt and began an apprenticeship as fireman's assistant on the railway. The honourable and not unexciting career of engine driver lay ahead of

him if he had persevered; but he gave up one form of transport for another, becoming a horse omnibus driver. A natural instinct for handling horses enabled him to manage with ease the teams of four or six in London's congested streets, and when, one day, a lead horse went mad and threatened to send the whole team berserk he knew just what to do. Crawling over the backs of the plunging beasts, he cut the demented one's throat—or so an unlikely family legend insists.

The memory of the recruiting sergeant lingered in his mind, however, and he determined to try again. Giving a false age, he managed to enlist into the 18th Hussars.

William Deller was made for the army, and the army for him. He loved everything about it; even the harsh discipline of those times. He excelled as a horseman. When his regiment moved to India he was able to distinguish himself at tent-pegging and the other horseback sports of that station. He began also to take an interest in physical training, for which he discovered a natural bent. Passing the necessary examinations, he was made an instructor, with sergeant's rank.

In 1895 the regiment returned from India. Walking out in London, Sergeant Deller met a nurse, Mary Cave, who worked at the Consumptive Hospital, Brompton, and lived with a sister in Mare Street, Hackney. She was small, placid, and pretty, with shining black hair and merry, dark sloe eyes; he was imperial, perfectly proportioned, his ramrod carriage adding illusory inches to his medium height. They made a striking couple, and they loved one another. They were married before the bugle and drum summoned Sergeant Deller away to South Africa to fight the Boers.

When the regiment returned from the war in 1902, Mary took rooms for herself and baby Emma opposite the barracks in Canterbury and Thomas contrived to spend much of his time with them in this first family home. But Canterbury lies in a hill-encircled hollow, through which runs the River Stour. Its vaporous atmosphere began to affect the baby, who had always been

'chesty'. When the doctor recommended Mary to move to some healthier place, William, rather than be parted from his wife and child again, sought and obtained his discharge from the colours, in 1903.

He was tremendously fit, and could have had many more years of useful and enjoyable service. The army and his family were all that mattered to him in life. He gave up the former for the latter, and spent the rest of his days regretting it.

They moved only a few miles from Canterbury, to Margate, more fashionable then than now and renowned for its bracing seaside air. At their little house in North-down Road Sergeant Deller, as he continued to be known, set up in the insecure practice of freelance physical training instructor. For a time he had a partner, Major Hayes, one of his former regimental officers; but the major withdrew after a few months and a brass plate was screwed on to the Dellers' front gate-post, reading 'Sergeant T. W. Deller, Swedish exercises, gymnastics'.

Margate and the Thanet coast have long been favoured sites for boys' and girls' colleges, and the Sergeant was soon busy building up a connection with as many of them as would engage him, bicycling from one to another to take an hour's physical jerks, a boxing lesson, a fencing class. The trim, taut figure, the cropped military haircut and perfectly disciplined moustache, the snow-white, unwrinkled drill vest bearing the crown and crossed cutlasses of the army physical training instructor, the smart cummerbund and razor-creased trousers: the combination of precisions which made up Sergeant Deller was soon a familiar and respected sight throughout the Thanet towns.

Even so, life was precarious for the Dellers. The Sergeant's work paid him well in terms of continued physical fitness, but in no other sense. His fees were necessarily low, yet slow in the payment, for the schools which employed him sent parents their bills term by term and had themselves to wait long periods for settlement.

Sergeant Deller did not get his share until every parent had paid up and his account could be settled complete. His tiny capital, augmented by a meagre income from private classes, had to carry the family economy meanwhile. They practised every possible economy, paying for nothing they could manage to do for themselves. The Sergeant, fortunately a gifted gardener, worked an allotment to grow the bulk of their food. He kept hens. He did all the shoe repairs in what he called his 'snobbing shop' in the garden shed. He swept the chimneys and undertook every kind of household make and mend. The school holidays, when he faced weeks of semi-idleness, were the worst times. Then, in addition to his customary early morning run or walk, he would spend the empty afternoons running by the hour, whatever the weather, returning flushed, but breathing as easily as when he had set out, for a soak in a hot bath and a rub down with liniment. He had always energy and to spare, but opportunities for earning a living by it were not his to make.

Mary gave her full share. If a few pence could be saved at the cost of an hour's hard work, saved they were. One of her children retains a vivid memory of coming home from school on winter afternoons, to find the kitchen dense with steam and his little mother, her pretty face scarlet and her hair saturated, pounding the clothes which boiled in the copper. She found time off from this incessant toil to bear seven children, four boys and three girls, in addition to having at least two miscarriages. When they were old enough to be useful the children helped with household tasks; but only those requiring minimum skill. With three daughters willing to relieve her, Mary never relinquished the cookery. She could not: there had never been time to teach any of the girls how to do it.

It was the Sergeant, with his tidy, military mind, who kept them from poverty. A less organized household might well have disintegrated into hopelessness and chaos. He appreciated each domestic problem as it arose, promptly taking the appropriate action to deal with it.

The children were sometimes allowed to go to see a silent film. Occasionally there would be no seats available at the afternoon performance in the tiny cinema, so they were permitted to go to the evening show, on condition that they were home by some strictly set time. Now and then, the fascination of the film would make them oblivious to the fact that the performance was over-running by a few minutes. Emerging at last, horrified to see the clock, they would run all the way home, arriving near to collapse but still a minute or two late. They knew what they would find: the Sergeant, watch in one hand, long black razor strop from the hook near the bathroom door in the other. Neither excuse nor apology could move him, as neither excuse nor apology could have saved any soldier running late on to the parade ground. The beatings he gave them were violent, sometimes close to savage. Mary Deller knew better than to intervene. One of her daughters remembers her standing as near to the child being punished as she dared, holding it, if she could, in reassurance, but never remonstrating with her husband. 'One's enough, Em,' she whispered once; and Emma understood that if her mother intervened, the blows would be turned on her too.

There were many rules to infringe. Talking at table was not allowed, and no one might rise until final Grace had been said. Newspapers and magazines were forbidden in the house. Absolute punctuality on every occasion was mandatory, and the summons of the Sergeant's piercing whistle had to be obeyed instantly by everyone within earshot.

Yet there was no insistence on early rising or physical jerks before breakfast. The Sergeant's outbursts were feared and resented, but his disciplinary demands were accepted as reasonable. He could be the kindest, most considerate of men, spending long hours in anxious attendance on any of them who fell sick. For all her apparent meekness and refusal to oppose him, Mary quietly ruled her Sergeant. He loved her intensely and relied upon her more than he knew. The worst times of all were when he would turn on her, and the children would tremble to hear his shouting from behind the closed bedroom door. Unreasoning jealousy brought out the worst in him. The most monstrous act of injustice, remembered still, followed Emma's return from her honeymoon. She only learned later that after she and her husband had departed the Sergeant had turned on Mary in a frenzy of abuse and accusation, and all because she had allowed Emma's husband to kiss her good-bye. Thereafter, whenever Mary went to answer the door to a tradesman the Sergeant would contrive to hover in the background, just to make sure that she was not 'carrying on' again.

Em herself had earlier found an effective way of dealing with one of her father's outbursts. Hearing him beating her brother Tom, she shouted, 'If you don't damn well stop hitting him, Dad, I'm going to fetch a policeman.' The threat, she knew, would have no effect: the oath would. The beating ceased at once. The Sergeant thundered down the stairs after Em, who wisely ran into the main street, aware that even uncontrollable temper could not make her father behave in an undignified way before strangers. Managing to give him the slip, she walked about for a time, hoping his temper would cool, before returning home and sneaking quietly into the kitchen, where her mother was nursing the latest baby. 'Mum,' she whispered, 'give me the baby to hold, then Dad won't be able to hit me.'

The baby she clutched in self-protection when the Sergeant entered was Alfred Deller.

*

He had been born on 31 May 1912, the youngest of the four boys. Alfred George Deller became known at once to the family as Young Alf, and still is.

By this time the family's finances were in a healthier state. Over the years the Sergeant's connections had snowballed. He now went further afield to take his classes, and close to the new home to which they soon moved in Arthur Road, Margate, there was a church hall which he was able to rent and use as a gymnasium. There was relative prosperity enough to make Alfred's childhood somewhat smoother and less restricted than that of his older brothers and sisters.

His first memory is of crying. He cried a great deal, at great length and very loudly. His worried mother decided to call the doctor. The doctor came, and Alfred cried for him. The doctor examined him, then turned to Mary with a laugh. 'No, Mrs Deller, there's nothing wrong with that boy. He has exceptional lungs, and he wants to exercise them. He cries for crying's sake.' So Alfred was left to develop his lungs in the way Nature had arranged for him.

He was a good little boy, with a touch of seriousness from the beginning. He was a little spoilt, compared with the rest, though he felt his share of the black razor strop. Looking back on his father, he considers that his demands were no more unreasonable, and his punishments no more unjustified, than was customary in most families of their class. In the Deller household you knew just where you stood, what you could or could not do, and what would happen to you if you defaulted. Like army life, it carried its own kind of certainty and security. The Sergeant bullied, but he protected. He enforced rigid discipline, and led his family securely and unitedly through the difficulties of years of near-poverty. He spared nothing of himself, and took no selfish pleasures. He was as hard as his muscles, and as unbending with himself as with others. The gentle, sweet Mary deserved a man capable of more tenderness than he; but she loved him, knew precisely how to handle him and, as a parent, provided exactly the counter-influence to his in their children's upbringing.

Having satisfied himself that all was proceeding tidily and smoothly according to his regulations, Sergeant

William Deller could march off the parade ground into watchful ease. Much of his spare time was occupied with ledgers and accounts, but he had a favourite relaxation, reading army drill manuals, the contents of which, though he must have known them by heart, never lost their fascination for him. He would sometimes instead read the Bible or Macaulay's *History of England*, both of which had accompanied him on his army travels, or, conscious of his lack of education, a dictionary. It was his boast that he had never read a novel. Like Mr Gradgrind, there was no room in his make-up for anything that was not unassailable, invulnerable fact. It was an attitude he shared with many of his generation, a Victorian equivalent of refusing to watch television 'on principle'.

Yet he had a keen sense of humour, even of fun. When he judged it the correct moment to do so, he would play on the floor with his children, his loud, barking voice drowning theirs and making the house ring with harsh noise. Mary unobtrusively covered her ears and, as at all times, made no complaint.

There was a small billiards table at which the Sergeant would play with his children. He bought a second-hand piano and let the girls have lessons. He played it himself, by ear, and bought himself a concertina, which he also contrived to master. Sometimes on Saturdays he would take Mary to music-hall at the Hippodrome, and their house windows often rattled to his bellowing of his favourite, 'Swing me up a little bit higher, Obadiah, do'.

One day, fulfilling a promise, the Sergeant returned home with a gramophone. Predictably, the records he bought with it were mostly of military marches, but there were some popular and sentimental songs, and another of his own favourites, 'The Laughing Policeman'. With the girls tinkling on the piano, the Sergeant, in good humour, roaring ditties to his own concertina accompaniment, and someone trying to listen to the gramophone, it was, in a cacophonous way, a musical household.

There is no substantial background of music, though.

As in so many families, there are vague stories of talented great-aunts and uncles; inevitably, perhaps, from a time that had seen so much home music-making. The Sergeant's mother is said to have had a better-than-average voice, while Mary's brother Alfred could play the violin noticeably better than most amateurs.*

When he stopped crying for a moment Alfred Deller must have been aware of the music around him. When he resumed crying it was sometimes to demand to be taken out to see 'the man with a stick on a piece of wood'. This turned out to be a street violinist whose appearance fascinated the child, though whether on account of his music, or the mechanics of the performance, nobody knows. But if Alfred Deller's musical inheritance was slight, and his father's contribution to it unmelodious, he acquired two things from the Sergeant which would prove to be amongst his chief assets as a singer. One of these was a splendid physique, with a great chest enclosing splendid lungs. The other was the rhythmic sense which has always been one of his most valuable possessions. 'My father had an incredible sense of rhythm,' he recalls. 'From my youngest days I used to go and watch him taking classes of twenty or thirty boys, swinging the Indian clubs while someone played the old piano in the corner of the gym. Father's sense of timing was faultless, and he would have the whole thing moving as precisely as a machine. It was the same when he exercised on the horizontal bars and the rings. He would swing and twist and somersault in perfect time. The rhythmic sense is, of course, as fundamental to music as it is to gymnastics, and I have always believed that I learnt the essentials of rhythm in my father's gym.'

When war came, two years after Alfred Deller's birth, the family suffered a severe setback. The Sergeant bore the first, cruellest shock of it when he hastened to enlist,

---

* The Austrian minor composer Johann Florian Deller (1729–73) is not known to have any link with the English family.

I I

and was rejected on the grounds of age. He was forty-two but fitter than most younger men and capable of playing an important part in their training. The best he could manage was to engage in recruiting, for which he was not given uniform to put on. One of the bitterest experiences of his life was being sneered at by strangers who, noting his trim figure, believed him to be a much younger man who had shirked active service.

The psychological blow to a man for whom the army was life itself, yet who could only stand helplessly on the sidelines of the war, was considerable. Even harsher, in practical terms, was the blow the war struck to his livelihood. Zeppelins appeared over Thanet in 1916, followed in 1917 by German bombers. Margate was shelled from the sea. Many boarding schools hastily closed their premises and moved to less vulnerable places, leaving the Sergeant with barely a handful of pupils. The connections he had built up were severed, with nothing to substitute for them. There was only one thing for him to do: he had to follow his pupils. Several of his schools had set up again in the Brighton area, so for months he travelled by train every day from Margate to Brighton, a journey of about a hundred miles, and back.

At their home in Arthur Road the family carried on, sitting out the air-raid warnings in their large coal cellar, which the Sergeant had equipped with benches. With money scarcer than ever, and six children on her hands, Mary worked even harder than before. When she did find time to relax, she built houses for them out of kindling wood and sometimes read to them. Her taste was for the romantic and sentimental: Harrison Ainsworth's historical romances of old London, Dickens in his more melting moments, tear-provoking stories by Victorian ladies about orphans in the storm. Most of all, she loved to read the serial stories from newspapers and magazines which, in the Sergeant's absence, she could enjoy in safety.

In time, even the Sergeant's stamina began to wilt

under the strain of so much travelling. He closed the Margate home, taking his family to live with him at a house in Hove, where he could be near his pupils and use the saved time by taking on still more. It was there that Young Alf, then aged four, first went to school and, soon after, appeared before an audience for the first time. Dressed in a sailor suit, he took part in a school concert, dancing a hornpipe and singing. It was a minor milestone indeed in his career, but one he remembers often when he performs today, some fifty years later:

'There was no sort of stage or dressing room, of course. We just performed on the classroom floor, and before it was our turn to come on we crouched down behind the old upright piano. I can still smell the dusty green cloth backing to the piano, as I waited there with the butter-flies fluttering in my stomach. It was the same nervous feeling that one gets before any kind of performance, and that musty smell comes back to me often today, when I'm waiting to go on.'

After the Armistice the family returned to Margate. The evacuated schools re-opened, and Sergeant Deller was once more in demand. The war years had hit him hard, but had not changed him. He was still fussing over untidiness or supposed slovenliness, and meting out the regulation punishment for the graver breaches of discipline, though not without opposition now from the older children. He had lost nothing of his energy or appearance. Every day he would weigh and measure himself. 'That tape-measure!' Mary murmured to a visitor, out of his hearing. But she understood his preoccupation. His physique and stamina were his only assets as a bread-winner. They repaid the close attention he gave them by providing the living. If he were to lose them, he and the family would be finished.

The family was now complete, from the oldest daughter, Emma, to Tom, Rose, Len, Horace, Alf and Grace. The older children were now able to look after the younger. Fortunately, they all got on well together.

Alfred found himself mostly in the care of his brother Horace, five years his senior. Like all the Deller boys they were fond of games, particularly football and cricket, and their good physique made them more than competent players. Horace and he would spend hours in a field practising diving catches with a cricket ball, or bowling to each other using wickets chalked on a wall. ('When Alf sent down a fast one there was a touch of the Larwood about him,' another former player recalls.) Horace was an ardent entrant in newspaper competitions. One year the *Daily Mail* organized a summer seaside competition featuring their children's cartoon character Teddy Tail, the Mouse. You had to create a design in the sand, working in some reference to Teddy Tail and, of course, the *Mail* and its popularity. Horace entered and employed Young Alf as his labourer, sending him running constantly to the rocks with a bucket to gather all the white stones he could find and quantities of different-coloured seaweeds. While Alf laboured, Horace painstakingly built up his design showing a lighthouse, with Teddy Tail peering from a window and the beams of the light cunningly incorporating the *Daily Mail*'s sales figure. He added a caption testifying to the newspaper's superiority above all others. At length, Alf having been graciously permitted to lay a few last pebbles and strips of black and green seaweed, the grand design was complete. A local photographer recorded it and the picture went off to Carmelite House. The Dellers' effort was declared the winning Margate entry and was rewarded by several of Lord Northcliffe's guineas.

Alfred was by this time attending Holy Trinity school, attached to the church which was to be destroyed in another war. He was a likeable little boy, neither exceptionally good nor noticeably bad. He was well built, more interested in games than in lessons, but with a serious, almost contemplative, side to his nature, too. He seemed to be quite incapable of understanding mathematics; but his English, which he liked best, was good. The music taught at Holy Trinity was of merely rudimentary type, but at his next school, Salmestone Elementary, where he went at the age of nine, the music teacher, Mrs Hiscock, was something of an enthusiast, and certainly discerning. Alfred had not been at the school many weeks when, one music period, she gave his class *Cherry Ripe* to sing. After they had completed the first verse, Mrs Hiscock stopped them and told Alfred to sing the next verse as a solo.

'I sang it,' he relates, 'and while I was doing so I was suddenly conscious for the first time that my voice sounded somehow different from the other chaps'. And there also came an intense pleasure, a feeling of happiness and joy. The fact that I was singing alone like that, and feeling such sensations, did something for me personally in a very deep way. I couldn't have described any of it in words, but I was very conscious of it. In a way, it was my beginning.'

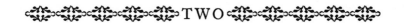

Music at Salmestone School was taught by ear. The class songbooks contained only the words, the tunes being picked up from Mrs Hiscock's playing. Alfred learnt them all very quickly, while remaining in complete ignorance of the meaning of musical notation.

When he was eleven his name was entered as a candidate for a place at Margate Boys' Central School. This new and forward-looking establishment, in fine surroundings, had been started after the war with a staff of ex-officers and progressive principles whose working out was already being watched with interest by many educational bodies. Competition for a place was keen, involving written and oral examinations. Alfred had worked hard at Salmestone and had hopes of succeeding, but for one obstacle: it was necessary to achieve a pass in mathematics. He sat the examination, and passed in everything—except mathematics.

Music and Mrs Hiscock came to the rescue. By one of those fortunate circumstances which have punctuated Alfred Deller's life, the headmaster of Margate Boys' Central School chanced to be Mr W. H. Hiscock, his music mistress's husband. He called Alfred in for an interview, gave him to understand that it was only because his wife had pleaded with him to make an exception on account of the boy's musical promise, and agreed to admit him, on condition that he worked hard to get his maths up to the required standard. Much as he would have liked to repay the gesture, Alfred never succeeded. Mathematics and all scientific and technical subjects eluded his grasp throughout school life, and have continued to do so ever since.

He worked well at other subjects, especially English, and while he never distinguished himself in any classroom subject, he did not discredit himself. The school's system relied much upon a sense of sportsmanship and fair play, and on co-operation between master and pupil. Merit marks were awarded for achievement, deducted for carelessness, laziness and unruliness. The worst penalty was to be known to one's house-fellows as the backslider who had let them down in the monthly merit shield competition. Alf Deller never let Gordon House down. Rather, he brought it credit in the sphere most certain to impress the greatest number of his fellows by being elected, in due course, captain of soccer and cricket and vice-captain of the school. A footballing team-mate, Cyril Macartney, remembers him as a 'gentle giant' of a right-back, hard and fearless in a tackle but using his strength only within the rules. His bellowed 'Right!', resounding across the field when he thought the ball was his, is still remembered. When Alf Deller played cricket, everyone watched. As well as being the leading fast bowler he was a prodigious hitter, putting many a ball out of the ground and into the housing estate near by.

The other thing that was beginning to distinguish him from the mass of his fellows was his singing. Again, he was fortunate in an encounter. The music master at Margate Central was Roy Monkcom, a man of Polish extraction, still in his twenties and a dedicated teacher. He sensed at once that Alfred was not only a better singer than most, but that he possessed a deep latent interest in music and was eager to learn.

'He took a great interest in me,' Deller says. 'He took me to my first concerts. They were a revelation. We had no radio in those days and no proper orchestral music or serious song on our gramophone records. No one could pretend that Margate has ever been a musical centre, and those concerts were no great shakes; yet they held me riveted. Then, when I'd barely got over the first sensations, Monkcom taught me how to listen properly. Even at the first concert he started telling me how to dig with my ears, as it were, underneath the predominant tune and listen for the other things going on at the same time. What he was doing, I came to realise later, was to distinguish for me the musical form and the counterpoint. It may sound a simple and obvious thing to do, but its effect on a boy of twelve who knew nothing about music was nothing short of a revelation. I found I could do as he suggested very easily, so that from then onwards I ceased to look at the "headlines" of a piece of music, but could absorb all the text together.

'I owe a great deal to Roy Monkcom. Shortly after I left the school he transferred to another outside Kent and I lost track of him, though I tried to get in touch. Many years later, when I had made something of a reputation, I was asked to sing in Handel's *Solomon* with the Reading Symphony Orchestra; and who should be leading the orchestra but Monkcom. It was a wonderful reunion.'

As well as learning something about music at school, Alfred was now singing regularly as a chorister at Margate Parish Church of St John the Baptist. Sergeant Deller had always insisted on regular attendance at church and Sunday School for all the children. Not all of them went gladly, but Alfred did.

From his very first Sunday afternoon visit to a service at Margate Trinity Church, when he was too young even to join the Sunday School, he had been sensitive to the atmosphere of church. Margate Trinity was a Low Church, with few mystical trappings to awe a small boy; but when his escorting sister showed him how to kneel, and he did so, with his nose only just reaching the ledge on which the hymnbooks lay, he smelt holiness, manifested in the cloth and glue of the hymnbook bindings.

After doing his share of singing from the family pew for several years, Alfred put his name down for the choir, after the choirmaster, Hector Shallcross, had written to the Central School asking for recruits. He was eleven, and therefore a good two years above the ideal age for starting to be a chorister, but he was still singing treble, and Shallcross agreed to hear him. 'Very well, I'll take you,' he agreed afterwards, 'but you're really too old to make a singer.'

Except that he was a rather old treble, the new chorister made no noticeable impact on his fellows or on the music. Although both Mrs Hiscock and Roy Monkcom had discerned in him a musical intelligence above the average, his promise seemed to extend little further. His singing was regarded with a certain respect by his school mates in tribute to an idol of the sports field. When he first appeared in a school concert, to sing the popular *Felix Keeps on Walking*, he had the audience thundering for more. Between that triumph and the next year's concert he had come under Monkcom's influence and developed more sober musical tastes, choosing for his second appearance the first Purcell air he was ever to sing to an audience, *I attempt from love's sickness to fly*. The entire school had greeted his arrival upon the stage with an ovation. When he gave them Purcell instead of Felix, he received what he terms 'the biggest raspberry of my career'.

At about this time he was promoted solo boy in the church choir. As such, he was invited to take part in a Sunday evening charity concert at the Margate Hippodrome, in a bill including conjurers, jugglers, and some comedy of a Sunday standard. Alfred wore his best suit, a plum colour, very fashionable at the time, which showed up spectacularly in the spotlight when he appeared for his solo number. The Sergeant and

Mary from their seat in the balcony heard someone pass a facetious remark about it. The Sergeant leaned across and growled, 'You wait till you've heard him sing.' But Alfred's choice was again far removed from the popular ditties of the day. The audience returned him respect, rather than enthusiasm.

He spent four quite happy years at Margate Central School. He enjoyed music and English, and managed to bumble along successfully in everything not involving science or maths. His all-round sportsmanship kept him in continuous respect. So did his physique. He was big and sturdy, and could hold his own with any antagonist, though he did not choose to do so by returning physical violence. From an early age, school bullying had incensed him. While his size and strength excluded him from becoming a victim, he discovered a gift for rescuing weaker boys by talking the bullies out of their intentions, to the point of making them ashamed of themselves.

He was a keen Scout, living all the year round for the annual camp near Canterbury. The private parkland, the lake, the big house, the tent life, the camp fire, the walk to the little church at Bishopsbourne for Sunday morning service, all added up to the most romantic experience he had known. He was a fittingly romantic figure, with his big build, jet-black hair and swarthy, almost gipsy-like complexion. His contemporary, Cyril Macartney, pays him a striking tribute: 'One of the few people you can remember clearly when you look at a school photograph forty years later.'

He left school at fifteen. He had been luckier than his brothers and sisters, none of whom had enjoyed secondary education. Now, he had to fall into line. The Sergeant, who had known insecurity ever since leaving the army, had no doubt about what constituted a safe job for an unqualified youth or girl. Each of his children was eased into some branch or other of retail trade. Tom and Len had gone into furnishing, Em into millinery, Horace, after a year of odd jobs at seven and sixpence a week, had broken the pattern by entering an estate agent's. Alfred was earmarked for furniture, but it was another chance circumstance that decided just where he would begin his apprenticeship. A few weeks before leaving school he had played for the cricket eleven against a team from Munro Cobb, the Margate furnishers. In the first innings he took seven wickets for eight runs, and seven for twenty in the second. He was promptly offered a job, accepted it, and played for the firm's team for many years.

He faced his future philosophically. For a year or more he had been aware of inner stirrings. So far as he could rationalize them, they added up to a vague ambition to do something in music: he did not know what. All he did know was that the family's financial position, although now rather better with several members working, did not allow for passengers. 'I saw my life in terms of doing some job which would earn me a living, while music would remain a valued spare-time pleasure and consolation. When that job turned out to be selling furniture, I thought to myself, "Well, it might just as well be this as anything."'

He started at Munro Cobb in 1927 at seven and sixpence weekly, to be increased by half a crown every six months. Striped trousers and a dark jacket and waistcoat were *de rigueur* to the dignity of even a junior apprentice salesman. He would be required to spend a year in hard furnishings, one in soft, and so on through the departments, learning and selling as he progressed. He found serving at the counter embarrassing, becoming a nightmare whenever the moment came for calculating the prices of lengths of cretonne at 1*s* 11½*d* a yard. Attempts to use a ready reckoner merely added to his confusion. But he was not one to stay depressed for long. Behind-the-scenes larking with the other apprentices could be relied on to drive off any lingering gloom.

The gift of mimicry which has helped to endear Alfred Deller to colleagues and friends throughout the world was evident even then. His best audience was female—Mr Munro Cobb's secretary and the cashiers. He was constantly in and out of their office with a new joke or impersonation. One afternoon, when Mr Cobb was out and no customers in sight, he noticed on a counter some Victorian fire-irons, beautifully polished, including a poker with an impressive knob on the end. A new Mayor of Margate had just been installed. Alfred dashed into the soft furnishing department to array himself in a colourful bedspread and a tea-cosy hat. Then, carrying the poker over his shoulder like a mace, he marched solemnly into the girls' office and reduced them to hysterics with a studied imitation of the Mayor making a speech of somewhat unmayoral character. Carried away by his eloquence, he did not pause to wonder why the girls' laughter had suddenly ceased. Mr Cobb, in the doorway behind him, cleared his throat. Fortunately, he was a boss who could share a joke.

There were several floors to the building, and a lift, beside each door of which was fitted a voice-pipe for inter-floor communication. You pulled out the plug and whistled to attract attention. Alfred achieved a perfect imitation of the wheezy whistle. The apprentices would wait until the old porter was polishing a floor at the far end of a department, then Alfred, hiding behind a piece of furniture, would whistle. Solemnly, the half-deaf man would put down his polisher and walk to the voice-pipe. His repeated ''allo?' was the confidently awaited pay-off.

One man at Munro Cobb for whom Alfred had nothing but deference was named Humphries. He was old, small, and wispy-haired, and resembled neither a sailor nor a poetry-lover. He was both. He had spent much of his life voyaging the world before the mast in sailing ships; and his greatest love was poetry. He and Alfred got talking about it. The old man had written verse of his own, and it was this natural, primitive work which 'opened the great flood-gates' of poetic mood and mystery for the youth. Once more, Alfred Deller had had a fortunate encounter. Poetry was to matter more to him than he or his old sailor mentor ever came near to sensing.

He worked six days a week for the firm, spending most of his spare time out of doors. His footballing talent at school had been spotted and he had been given a trial for Margate Town Boys, which gained him a place in the team as full-back, leading in turn to selection for a trial game in the Kent Boys' team. In the summer months he played cricket for Margate. Off the sports field he was a Rover Scout and a member of the church youth organization, the King's Messengers.

Keeping up a connection with his school as a member of a little band which attended the Old Boys' Association dances, Alfred played the drums, the first instrument he ever mastered. Becoming ambitious, he managed to buy a banjolele and learnt it easily. He was also slowly teaching himself to play the family piano.

A nightly custom, amusing or irritating to its regular witnesses, prevailed in the Deller household. At a certain hour the Sergeant would gravely draw out his watch, consult it for some moments, then say to Mary, 'Coming, mother?' Every night, Mary would answer, 'I don't know as I feel like going.' She and everyone else in the room knew what the Sergeant's reply would be: 'Well, we'd better get going, then.' Then they would rise, put on their outdoor clothes, and walk down to an old public house near by, the Sergeant for one glass of beer, Mary for a stout. They were not gossips who could make friends readily: the Sergeant's dignity and pride restrained him from reaching out to strangers. But they would chat a little to other customers of the pub, amongst them an old lady whose husband, it transpired, was an invalid who gave piano lessons for one shilling a time. The Sergeant offered to send Young Alf, who remembers:

'I went about six or eight times. The old man was partially paralysed. He'd sit at the end of this terrible old walnut-cased piano, chain-smoking. I remember the great brown stains on his fingers, and the shaking hand holding the cigarette with the ash just managing to balance on the end. He tried to teach me *The Bluebells of Scotland* before some financial crisis brought the visits to an end. If you can call that tuition, it was all the tuition I ever had. I taught myself the rest, so, of course, my fingering is all over the place. My Bach playing, they tell me, is highly eccentric.'

His voice, in his mid-teens, was overdue to break, and there was no guarantee that he would find himself with a good adult one. Music of some sort seemed to be necessary to him, and his natural sense of pitch and interval, polished by regular choir work, gave good promise of success on some instrument or other. His teacher, Roy Monkcom, had suggested shortly before he left school that he try the violin. A dozen or more years after he had ceased to cry for 'the man with a stick on a piece of wood', Alfred began to save up the two pounds ten shillings needed for an old one Monkcom had found in a pawnshop. He asked his parents if, instead of giving him presents at Christmas and his birthday, they would put a little money aside for him. The shopkeeper agreed to reserve the fiddle, and in due course, and by many means, the money was raised, plus twelve and six for a bow. His sister Em, visiting Walworth Market in London one day with her husband, saw a music-stand for sale for half-a-crown. They bought it and carried it off to Margate for Alfred to use. He had started working by then, and could manage to find one and sixpence a time for lessons from a Mr Dyer.

He studied the violin for three years. He worked hard and picked it up naturally and quickly; but he soon found that violin-playing could never be more than a pastime. His fingers are long, except for the vital fourth finger of the left hand, which is disproportionately short. The G string was a difficulty for him from the beginning, and he could never manage it with facility. Still, he managed to become proficient enough to play the second part in the

Bach Double Concerto. His mother made him a bag of green baize, tied round the neck with a black tape, for carrying the violin, until Tom found, in a junk shop, a battered old coffin-type case, bought and renovated it and presented it to his brother. Almost every member of the family, at one time or another, contributed somehow towards the gifted boy's progress. Deller still has the violin, disintegrated but precious.

So, when he played at the Old Boys' dances, it was on the violin, with a repertoire ranging from the Palm Court kind of music to what was loosely called jazz. Another violinist, known as 'Squeaker' Evans, who heard him and was impressed, suggested that he might pick up some welcome cash by joining his trio, to play two nights a week in one of Margate's many small hotels during the summer season. Alfred did so and fulfilled a few engagements, not caring much for the music but glad to have the money. Glad, that is, to anticipate having the money, for

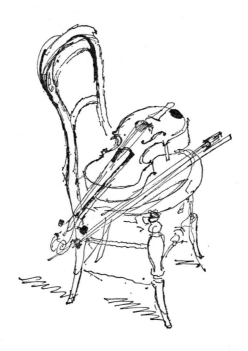

when reckoning time came Squeaker was full of excuses but empty of cash. He proposed a settlement in kind. His father was a dealer in second-hand goods. If Alfred would care to go to the shop he could take his pick from several real leather, shaped violin cases. He did, and found himself professionally equipped at last.

He was not sorry that the job with the trio had folded up. Music, to him, was becoming something to be taken with increasing seriousness. He was very conscious of the dignity of the calling of musician, even if it was, in his case, only a spare-time adjunct to furniture selling. One evening he and Horace went to a local cinema in the High Street, where a film about the life of Liszt was being shown. The film was silent, the music for the appropriate piano passages being provided by the cinema pianist who strummed the usual accompaniment to the film. Alfred sat fascinated by his fellow musician's skill, and, when the film was over, marched down to the front, leaning over the brass rail and curtain which concealed the pianist from the audience to bestow warm praise, from one musician to another. When his brother asked him who he thought he was to make such pronouncements he replied that it had never occurred to him to wonder. The pianist had deserved praise: he had praised him.

The chief part of Alfred Deller's music-making, though, remained his work with the choir of St John the Baptist. He had quickly made a reputation as a soloist which had extended to various local concert platforms. At nearly sixteen he was still singing soprano. The choirmaster was baffled. In accordance with the belief that over-use of a boy's voice might be detrimental to his singing as a man, Mr Shallcross called Alfred to him and told him he had better leave the choir.

The disappointment was tremendous, but the boy respected his choirmaster's knowledge of what was best for him. He sang for the last time at the parish Christmas party. One or two speeches were made in his praise. The vicar presented him with an inscribed silver watch. With a heart full of sadness at the thought that this might, for all he knew, mark the end of his days as a chorister, Alfred Deller made his way homeward.

THREE

If Margate was not exactly the hub of the musical universe, it was a thriving centre of entertainment of most other kinds. The charming little Georgian Theatre Royal had been closed since 1915 and would not re-open until 1930; but, in 1927, the Hippodrome flourished as the summer venue for all the top West End successes, with their original stars. During the winter, when audiences were harder to find, vaudeville and revue took over. Plays were presented at the Winter Gardens. Pierrots, concert parties and minstrels—the latter including the famous Uncle Bones and his troupe—flourished on the pier and elsewhere.

There was plenty of amateur entertainment, too. At the very moment that Alfred Deller was taking his sad farewell of the choir, another Margate resident, a Mr Crawshaw, charged with organizing evening entertainments in connection with a week's trade exhibition at the Winter Gardens, was looking for amateur acts to make up an all-male Nigger Minstrel bill. He had his tap-dancers, his cross-talk act, his interlocutor and enough minstrels to fill the stage nicely. All that remained was to select carefully the four voices for the quartet to sing the sentimental ballads essential to such a show. He had heard young Deller sing and thought his high voice would be ideal for the quartet's top line. He found Alfred willing, and within a few weeks the show was on, with a blacked-up Alfred Deller singing with the quartet in *Sweet and Low* and its like, and taking a solo spot with *Love's Old Sweet Song*, singing everything in the only way he knew how to sing, alto. Every night his solo got a tremendous hand. On the Saturday night, after the final show, he was removing his blacking in the dressing-room when Hector Shallcross appeared at his elbow, solemn-faced and shifting from one foot to the other.

'Well, Alfred, you're singing as well as ever. I don't understand it, but I can't lose you. *We* can't lose you. You'll have to come back to the choir and sing a bit of alto.'

So he returned to the choir stalls of the Church of St John the Baptist, no longer, now, standing in the front row with the boy sopranos, but behind and at the end; no longer singing the top line of the music, but the second, alto line. He knew nothing of the countertenor voice, its technique, historical background or tradition. He merely sang in his natural way, the same way, basically, in which he still sings today.

'Many boys who sing, if they produce a bright, forward tone, are using a type of pharyngeal falsetto, with a head voice, not off their full vocal chords,' he explains. 'In fact, the boys don't use that part of the voice for singing which they use for shouting. When they see someone across a field, and call, "Hi, old so-and-so!", they produce a voice, as singers say, "off the chest". But when they sing they use this pharyngeal head quality.

'This is what I did then, and still do now. When I went back into the choir as an alto, instead of a soprano, there was no change at all in the way I used my voice. I merely sang the second line instead of the top. After a while, of course, I found that, singing at a lower *tessitura*, I had to use lower notes and not the upper fourth or fifth of my voice. It meant that I had to go down quite often to the ledger-lines below middle C, below G, and so on. This caused me some worry, because although I could produce those low notes, I couldn't give them any real resonance. The sound was inclined to disappear when I got round about the A or even B below middle C. I couldn't get any real bite.

'There was no one to whom I could turn to ask about it; and, if there had been, they wouldn't have known. So I simply had to evolve my own method of extending the resonance of my voice downward, and I now know that what I did by instinct and nature was the correct thing. This was to use all the forward sinus resonators and to take the voice, step by step, downward; moving from the head register I had used as a boy down into the chest register.

'This was really the point where my life as a counter-tenor began, as a boy of sixteen to seventeen singing simple alto parts in the church choir.'

Side by side with this instinctive change in his vocal technique there emerged suddenly a new awareness of music in the context of life, both in the personal and the broader sense. It made a deep and lasting impression on him.

'At that time the musical repertoire of the church depended very much on the Victorian composers. Not long after I returned to the choir Lent approached and Mr Shallcross started to prepare us for a series of mid-week services. One piece of music he chose as appropriate to the season was Orlando Gibbons' motet, *O Lord, increase my Faith*. Now, until this time I had known nothing of Tudor church music, let alone of Orlando Gibbons. One Friday evening we went through this motet for the first time, and I'm sure our first attempt was a pretty bad one. But as I sang my part it suddenly felt as though a door had been opened in Heaven. I had a sensation of immediate and complete fulfilment; and as we reached that marvellous combination of the music and the words in the last page I knew certainly that from that moment the music of this period would be my life.

'It would be many more years before I would sing such music at all frequently. But I think that experience placed me in the true centre of my life. I have believed since then that life can only make sense within a spiritual context; that everything is related to the spiritual, and that the arts are an extension of man's spiritual nature. This was the first inkling I had of it, and it was a most incredible feeling.'

Another experience, outside the church this time, added to this sense of revelation.

'It happened one November night. I had just left a choir practice at which we had been preparing carols for Christmas from a new volume called the *New English Carol Book*. It was a night of bright moonlight, and frost was gleaming on the road and the fences and gates of the houses as I walked through the unromantic council-housing estate at Margate, where we had moved into one of the first houses to be completed. As my footsteps rang in the stillness there was going through my head the tune of one particular carol:

> As up the wood I took my way
> The night began to fall,
> And all around the snow lay white
> And I heard a sweet voice call.

'Suddenly—and I could point out even now the very spot where this happened—I was overwhelmed by a feeling of joy and complete happiness of indescribable intensity. I felt that whatever might happen to me in life would be for the best; that something had, as it were, taken me over completely and was going to organize my life to be everything that I wished it to be. It was an amazing feeling of exaltation, shot through with a pure joy that I have only felt once since, and that many years later. Often, in times of stress and anxiety, I have recalled that experience and been comforted immediately.'

The feeling for poetry, kindled and fanned by old Mr Humphries, was intensifying, too. Another boy, Fred Crispe, also a violinist, with whom he played duets, shared his fondness for such things. They would take long walks together on winter's nights, along the Cliftonville cliffs to Kingsgate, with the wind driving them forward and the sea spray sheeting up over the cliff edge. It was as near to romantic intensity as one could aspire at Margate, and he would return home in the grip of it all and write verses of his own:

> A Jay and a Magpie adazzle the winter sun
> And shake the stark fingers of the lichened tree
> Dancing a pattern on the heavy earth.
> A shaft of swift perception pierces the Time-Locked door
> And I am oned in the perfect dance of the eternal now.

On a less exalted level he went on playing his fiddle at the Old Boys' hops, and, eager for every kind of musical experience, took up someone's suggestion that he might join the Margate Amateur Opera Group. Arriving at the hotel where rehearsals for an operetta, or some such work, were in progress, he was interviewed by a harassed musical director.

'What do you sing?'

'Alto.'

'Alto! Oh, well, get over there amongst the girls.'

He never attended again.

In 1929 a blow fell which knocked mere musical preoccupations into second place: he got the sack. The depression had set in. Kindly old Mr Munro Cobb, hating the circumstances which had forced him to do it, called Alfred in one day and explained as gently as he could that economies had to be made and the junior staff with no wives or children to support must be the first to go.

Much as he hated joining the Labour Exchange queue to draw the dole, Alfred soon had cause to be thankful

32

for the few shillings it brought in each week. Four months passed by with no other job in sight and the deepening depression making it less and less likely that one would ever come his way. Then, in the seventeenth week, yet another of those seemingly chance circumstances which have directed his life came to his rescue and set another course for his destiny.

A member of the St John the Baptist church congregation had invited a friend from St Leonard's-on-Sea, adjoining Hastings, to spend a weekend at Margate, and took him along to a church social function at which Alfred sang several solos. The visitor, who happened to be sub-organist of Christ Church, St Leonard's, was much impressed. He approached the young soloist afterwards to ask if he would object to his mentioning him to his organist, Dr Allan Biggs, a member of the well-known musical family. Christ Church, he added, was a wealthy and influential church, and there was a good chance that if Alfred were accepted for the choir a job could also be found for him. The offer was gladly accepted.

In due course a letter arrived, inviting him to spend a weekend at Hastings, and a few days later he found himself a guest in the house of a Miss Jakeham, a pillar of Christ Church. It was a household in the Dickensian style, lit by open gas jets without mantles. Miss Jakeham, a semi-invalid of great gentility, lay on her couch all day attended by a manservant with a vast handlebar moustache and an unchanging expression of deep gloom, who brought her constant relays of hot-water bottles. She loved talking to young men and was soon assuring Alfred of her influential support. Christ Church was, and still is an advanced Anglo-Catholic church. High Mass that Sunday was a new experience for Alfred, the liturgy and atmosphere fascinating him immediately. After the service he went up into the organ gallery to sing, to Allan Biggs' accompaniment, for the Rector, Father Roberts. By the time he had finished Father Roberts' face was radiant. 'We *must* have you,' he declared. 'We will do all we possibly can to get you here.'

Alfred returned to Margate and the dole. Every day he waited eagerly for the postman, and every day there was nothing from St Leonard's. Then, one afternoon while he was pottering in the garden shed, knocking together some props for an amateur dramatics production, his mother came down the path, apprehensively fingering the buff envelope of that rare form of communication with the Deller household, a telegram. Trembling almost as much as she, Alfred ripped it open. It read, 'COME TO CANTERBURY NEXT WEEK FOR INTERVIEW FOR POSSIBLE JOB IN HASTINGS.'

Why he should have been summoned to Canterbury was explained when he found himself being interviewed at Lefevre's department store by the chairman-director of the Drapery Trust, another of whose businesses was the large general furnishing house of Plummer Roddis at Hastings.* Alfred was offered a salesman's job with this firm, to start in a few weeks' time. He accepted. Looking for a temporary job for him in the meantime, Allan Biggs approached the much smaller firm of Elijah Gray & Sons, Ltd, Complete House Furnishers and Undertakers, 138, London Road, St Leonard's-on-Sea. On that very day, as it happened, the firm's salesman had gone down with scarlet fever: the offer of a temporary hand was accepted with alacrity. Once more, unbeknown to him, Fate had set Alfred Deller upon one of the major paths of his life.

He went to live in Hastings feeling himself to be a marked man. Life's obliging way of opening a door whenever another had closed behind him had not escaped his notice. He had no doubt at all who was responsible. God had shown Himself unto young Alf Deller. He was humbly grateful, awed, yet determined not to play the

---

* Readers familiar with H. G. Wells's *Kipps* may have noticed certain similarities between young Kipps and young Deller. An added coincidence is that it was by Plummer Roddis (Folkestone branch) that Kipps was employed.

hypocrite about it. If God had picked him out to be one of His musicians, then a musician he was going to be seen to be. Disregarding the fact that God had arranged primarily for him to sell furniture at thirty-five shillings a week plus commission on sales, with part-time singing in addition for another twenty-six pounds a year, he hastened off to a chain store to select a black, double-breasted coat, reaching almost to his ankles, a black, broad-brimmed hat of the style reputedly favoured by assassins and anarchists, and a black-and-white silk polka-dot choker. Thus arrayed, he arrived in Hastings, and the populace wondered.

He found good lodgings, with full board and part of his laundry included, for twenty-five shillings a week, which left a gratifying weekly balance. A little later he moved to share rooms with two young and jolly veterinary assistants, lodging next door to the shop. They made a high-spirited trio and one of the others, Rodney Pickett, has remained a life-long friend. A few weeks after arriving, Alfred had moved over to Plummer Roddis as arranged. He found he was required to live in with the other salesmen, and hated it. After a week he returned to Elijah Gray's, and his destiny.

Elijah Gray had founded the family firm in the previous century. On his death it had passed to his seven sons and one daughter. Possessing more commercial acumen than any combination of her brothers, the daughter had bought them out one by one and now exercised sole control over the flourishing little firm. She had parted from a charming, artistic, but unreliable husband, named Lowe, when her only child, Peggy, was still quite young. For nearly ten years since she had devoted herself to her business and her daughter, and maintained a completely platonic companionship with an old friend, a kindly married man whose wife was permanently confined in an institution.

Peggy, at the time of Alfred's arrival, was about his own age, a trim, vivacious little blonde, working as secretary to the editor of the local newspaper, the *Hastings*

Observer. She was as startled as everyone else by the new arrival's mode of dress, but quickly recognized that the affectation sprang from ingenuousness, not conceit, and that there was more to him than met the eye. Her mother saw it, too, and it worried her. She found his charm immense, his high spirits and ready flow of good talk instantly disarming, his manly build and dark good looks fascinating. Having herself fallen for a charmer, to her cost, she was determined that her daughter should make no such mistake. Before long, she was taking every care to keep her attractive young salesman well in his place. It was made clear that he would be 'Deller', the junior shop-hand, and nothing more. And, as she admitted to him years later, a stronger reason for her restraint towards him developed with time, as instinct told her that Deller would sooner or later have to choose between the security of settled employment and the hazards of professional life. There were plenty of music-lovers amongst her customers ready to tell Mrs Lowe that her employee's talents were of no common order.

Hastings was, and to a large extent still is, one of the leading musical centres of the provinces. The resident Municipal Orchestra, under its permanent conductor Julius Harrison, gave symphony concerts every Friday evening, Sunday afternoon and Sunday evening, with a 'pop' on Saturday evening. World-famous artists appeared with it, and in course of time, and for an expenditure of sixpence a seat, Alfred heard playing of a kind he had never known before by such soloists as Casals, Rachmaninov and other artists of lesser fame.

Christ Church possessed a magnificent Willis organ, and, in Dr Allan Biggs, one of the best organists in the country. Easter Day, when the strings and timpani of the Municipal Orchestra would join the choir in the west gallery for a Haydn or Mozart Mass, always produced an indelible impression on Deller. Equally, Biggs was an authority on plainsong, having helped to edit the first English manual. All the great chants for Holy Days were performed at Christ Church, with, to Deller, unforgettable effect and more than a touch of influence upon his own singing.

'I found I had a natural affinity with plainsong,' he says. 'I have never ceased to feel that the singing of Gregorian chant should be part of the basic training of all singers. You are not bound to a bar-line. You are free to float along on those great, long-flowing phrases. I think that, imperceptibly, the singing of plainchant early in my career affected my approach to phrasing, quite apart from the other effects this finest form of church music had on me.'

The beauty of its liturgy, for which Christ Church was renowned, and the new-found attraction of the Catholic form of worship there, overwhelmed Deller's romantic soul. He was tempted instinctively to commit himself all the way by joining the Roman Catholic church. After examining the prospect keenly and thinking deeply, however, he found himself unable to accept the tenet of absolute papal authority, so let the idea drop. The Anglo-Catholic attitude, both in its degree and its historical background, he found entirely satisfactory. One of the first of a succession of clergymen who have had a cumulative influence on Alfred Deller's life was a priest at Christ Church at the time, the late Lance Mellor, founder of the Christ Church Homes for homeless children. He had a wonderful sense of humour, always organizing the Christmas pantomime and taking the Dame's part. Speaking of him, Deller uses an expression often echoed in other people's references to himself: 'He really lived his Christianity out to the full; not only in church, but carrying it through into his whole life.'

Father Mellor's magnetic personality quickly drew Deller into many of his youth activities. He became a keen member of the Christ Church Younger Community. They met in friends' houses to listen to lectures, discuss and read plays. This led to the formation of the Christ Church Dramatic Society, with Alfred Deller, of the persuasive tongue and commanding confidence, as producer. One of their first productions was *The Eternal Spring*, a three-act situation comedy about an archaeologist who marries his secretary for the sake of convenience, and falls in love with her later. The part of Nockles, 'a suave and efficient butler', was played by the producer, his first appearance on the dramatic stage; and the leading role of Mary, the 'charming yet unsophisticated' secretary, was acted impressively by Peggy Lowe. Despite her mother's determination to keep her well away from the young salesman, amateur dramatics and religion began to bring her daughter into frequent contact with the dangerous charmer. Although she had done no acting before, Peggy had accepted with enthusiasm his suggestion that she join the Christ Church Players. Her lively personality had quickly made its mark on the company and its audiences, so that she generally found herself in a leading rôle. She had not been a regular churchgoer previously, but now began to attend every week and took Confirmation. Circumstances had also decreed that she and Alfred should see a good deal of one another during their daily work, for Peggy had by now left her job at the newspaper to act as her mother's secretary.

Mrs Lowe took firm steps to counteract any possible effects of this increased proximity. In Deller's first months with the firm he had been treated to outings in the family car, with Mrs Lowe driving and Peggy as his fellow passenger, tea at some point on the journey, and a pleasant, polite chatter all the way. Now, these jaunts ceased. Deller's morning greetings to his employer were returned coldly, if at all, and conversation confined strictly to business. Mrs Lowe's discouraging tactics were at first less necessary than she supposed. Peggy liked Alfred well enough, but was by no means smitten. She was attractive, popular, the daughter of a well-to-do, respected family, and consequently did not lack other admirers whose background and means contrasted markedly with those of a young shopman. At one stage her mother deliberately set out to encourage other young men, some of them with cars of their own, to squire Peggy about, giving her unlimited time off from her desk for the purpose. Often, Deller watched from behind the counter as Peggy ran out with her swimming things, to be driven off in a sports car. The feeling this provoked was not quite one of pain; he had not set his cap at Peggy. Yet, deep down, each recognized a mutual attraction and found it intensifying. Alfred had always got on well with the other sex. He had had plenty of girl friends; but this time he felt differently. For her part, Peggy tried to rationalize herself out of whatever it was she seemed to be feeling for him, only to come up against the notion that there was an indefinable something more to him than to any of the other young men. He bought her flowers and wrote poems to her—even if he did use the backs of linoleum tiles for the purpose. Without going so far as to declare their feelings for one another, the young couple tacitly acknowledged them. To placate Mrs Lowe they agreed to spend less time together outside working hours, and see what effect it produced.

The effect on Alfred surprised him. Admitting to himself what he had never before allowed himself to believe, that he had been on the brink of love and marriage, he thought he recognized another of God's emphatic signals. Yes, there it was, perfectly clear: God had earmarked Alfred Deller for a priest. He went for counsel to the priests at Christ Church. They were at once pleased and encouraging. He was serious-minded, fervently identified with the church in both its spiritual and social rôles, and the possessor of mature gifts of understanding and compassion. They assured him of their support for his candidature, but, suddenly, instinct made him draw back. He had been mistaking emotional reaction for true vocation. Still, he wavered for several months before asking Peggy to go about with him again. She was as relieved as he: they acknowledged their love.

One evening, when he had seen Peggy back to the foot of her stairs, the landing light snapped on and Mrs Lowe appeared, grim-faced.

'Go to bed, Peggy,' she ordered. 'I want to speak with Deller.'

He went up apprehensively and took a seat in the drawing-room. At once, to his deep embarrassment, his employer began to cry, pouring out recriminations on him for wishing to take an only daughter away from a lonely woman. He, reasonably, replied that she was depriving a lonely man of a wife. Then the tears ceased, but as she saw him to the door, Mrs Lowe added, 'I can't depend that you aren't going to run off at the first opportunity to go on with this mad singing business.' Deller returned to his lodgings feeling too bewildered to know whether to be happy or dejected.

Eventually Mrs Lowe resignedly accepted defeat. Although her future son-in-law remained plain 'Deller' in the hearing of customers, in private the surname was dropped, though not in favour of his christian name: intimacy was signified by his being addressed as nothing at all. Materially, the signs were much more encouraging. Having capitulated, Mrs Lowe suddenly found she could not do enough to help. Deller's salary was increased. He was regarded as shop manager. An uncle of Peggy's, a master builder, began construction of a nice house for them in a pleasant part of St Leonard's.

In the quietness of his room, Deller took stock of his situation. The prospect was far from alarming. He had never known security. He had no capital and had never earned much more than his living and modest pleasures demanded. He was about to step up to a respected level of the community, with a house, a good salary with a position of authority, and, not least, a wife whom he loved deeply. The business of Elijah Gray & Sons Ltd. was well-established, with the satisfactory turnover for those days of some £9,000 a year, and Mrs Lowe had made it quite clear that it would eventually be left to Peggy and himself. Meanwhile, she was insisting upon giving them all they needed in the way of furnishings and other household necessaries.

The thought that he might be selling such things to other people for the rest of his days did not daunt him. Only the lesser part of him seemed to be involved in the business, whose demands he met automatically. It also brought him into pleasant contact with all sorts of people. He was frequently out of the shop, visiting people's homes to estimate for carpets and curtains, and advise on furnishings. Often, an absence would extend hours longer than the needs of duty. Mrs Lowe fretted and fumed, 'Where has that man got to?', knowing full well that he and his customers would be engrossed in some conversation on any topic under the sun except their furnishing problems. So, his working life was tolerable, even pleasant. As to music, things were moving encouragingly enough. Dr Biggs was a friend of Mrs Lowe, who willingly met his requests that Deller should have time off on all saints' days to sing in the church. When Biggs went to some other parish to give a special recital or inaugurate a new organ he usually took Deller with him as special soloist. The Press had begun to notice him: 'Mr Alfred Deller (a remarkable male alto)'; 'Mr Deller, the eminent alto.' 'A most impressive feature of the evening was the surprising quality and perfect control of Mr Alfred Deller's alto voice, which has unlimited power combined with the greatest delicacy. His rendering of "O Thou that tellest" and "He shall feed his flock", was an experience not to be forgotten by the large congregation.'

Not all his notices had been quite impartial. Allan Biggs happened also to be the music critic for the *Hastings Observer* and a local correspondent for the *Morning Post* (now the *Daily Telegraph*). Still, it was gratifying to a singer of nineteen to read any sort of praise, and when he sang in places other than church, where applause was in order, his audiences left him in no doubt of the sincerity of what Biggs had written. His biggest chance yet had come in an invitation to sing at one of the Municipal Orchestra's concerts. He performed two groups of English songs with piano. 'The sensation of this concert,' ran the newspaper report, 'was the appearance of Alfred Deller, the possessor of an alto voice of almost incredible beauty. He astonished the enthusiastic audience in two groups of Old English songs by the total absence of effort with which he used his voice, which is capable of infinite light and shade from a full, rich tone down to a mere whisper. It is a long time since we heard anything as touching as his singing of "Willow, Willow", "Drink to me only", and the other examples of fine English songs which he gave. Mr Deller's intonation and articulation are as perfect as the way he produces those silvery tones, unusual enough in a lady, but in a man, phenomenal.' Even if Allan Biggs had written it, it was no more than the truth. Deller appeared many more times at the White Rock Pavilion, and sang in many more churches. In an article on 'Hastings as music centre' in the *Morning Post*, Richard Capell, paying tribute to the distinction of Christ Church choir's work under Allan Biggs, concluded,

'The Christ Church Choir possesses an alto soloist whose match one could go far without finding.'

Years earlier, young Alf Deller had confided to a sister-in-law his burning desire to set foot on the ladder of musical progress. A decade had passed since then. His technique and understanding of music had developed side by side. He had made a small name in a limited district. As he sprawled in his room now, taking stock of his life on the eve of marriage, he knew that the odds in favour of his becoming widely renowned were slight. He was twenty-five. Many celebrated soloists had been noticed well before that age. Apart from the guidance of choirmasters he had had no musical training, had attended no conservatoire: what he knew he had found out for himself. His voice, moreover, was of the rarest and least useful kind. The male alto voice, as generally known, was a curiosity of limited ability, little art, and associated with that unpleasant hooting sound, heard only fleetingly above the more manly voices, which had gained it the label of 'owl-to'. There could be little prospect of solo work for such a voice; and what there was would be in a class of music that would appeal only to an esoteric minority.

Yet, though these were familiar thoughts to Alfred Deller, they had never managed to depress him. When he sang Sterndale-Bennett's *O Lord, Thou hast searched me out*, he expressed his own conviction. Some weeks later, visiting the half-built house with Peggy, he was seized with sudden panic. Were they building him a prison? He blurted out, 'Peggy, I hope you'll understand this: although there's no sign of anything at present, you must know that if my chance to get on as a singer ever does come up I may feel I have to go after it without thought for anything else.'

Peggy replied, 'Don't worry. We'll live it as it comes.'

They were married on 5 June 1937.

FOUR

The wedding took place, of course, at Christ Church, conducted by Father Frank Steel. There was a full nuptial mass, Palestrina's *Aeterna Munera Christi*, and the whole occasion, on a scorching day, seemed as magnificent as a coronation through which Peggy passed, friends reported later, with a fixed smile and a glazed stare. They went off to honeymoon near Honiton, Devon, at a pleasant little hotel on the River Otter, from which guests were invited to catch their own trout for breakfast. After a blissful week they returned to St Leonard's, where their house was ready for them to move in, and Alfred squared himself to face his future as a businessman.*

It was at this time that he began to be deeply concerned about social questions. The Christian observances which gave him such deep spiritual and romantic satisfaction had somehow ceased to be enough. 'I felt that if Christianity really meant anything at all it should be lived out in practical terms of sociological work,' he says. 'If we believe that Christ is the Incarnate Son of God, then the logical implication of the Incarnation is that all of life, everything in life, is sanctified through Christ. The heart of all degrees of Catholicism is the Blessed Sacrament. I had gradually come to see that the presence of our Lord in the Sacrament means that the whole of life *is* sacrament: that everything in our relationships with one another, in our politics and in our social work, is sanctified. I felt this very strongly. Some of my views were called "Bolshie" by certain people who believed the church should keep out of everything except its spiritual func-

---

* An additional argument with which Mrs Lowe had tried to dissuade Peggy from marrying him has been reflected throughout his career in a mistaken belief about the physical make-up of a singer with so high a voice. 'He's not a complete man, you know,' she had warned her daughter. It is enough to relate that a few months after their marriage Peggy began her first pregnancy. They now have two sons and a daughter.

tions. In a sense, I suppose they were right. My attitude in those days may have been a sort of Christian communism; it was certainly nothing to do with political Communism.'

He became an active worker for his beliefs, encouraged by his rector and enthusiastically supported by Peggy and their fellow members of the Christ Church Young Group. The church was situated in a poor district of mean back streets, in which many old people lived in wretched conditions. The young men and women of Christ Church went round to clean up for them and, with paint and wallpaper, tried to repair the dilapidations of age and neglect. It was their practical gesture. Otherwise, their activities consisted mainly of discussions amongst themselves. Regular Sunday evening meetings were held, with guest speakers invited by Alfred. A Fascist spoke to them one week, a Communist the next. The members discussed both points of view and then, on the third Sunday, the speakers were invited to come back and join them in listening to the Christian sociological point of view, expressed by Father W. G. Peck, at that time principal of the Industrial Christian Fellowship.

They also discussed pacifism. Alfred's feelings about it had long roots. His childhood had been passed under the stern rule of a man for whom militarism was the supreme creed. Sergeant Deller's notion of conducting a good conversation was to repeat for the umpteenth time the familiar yarns of his experiences in India and South Africa. 'Boast, boast, boast!' a daughter-in-law remembers Mary whispering as they passed in the doorway with tea things while the Sergeant held forth in the parlour. That same daughter-in-law, Mrs Beatrice Deller, describes the whole family, the Sergeant excepted, as people incapable of hurting even a beetle.

Alfred Deller also recalls the effect on him as a boy of his parents' overheard quarrels. He would lie in bed terrified by their shouting, fearful that the next thing he would hear would be blows. It made all violence a distasteful, degrading thing. At the cinema he had seen *All Quiet on the Western Front, Hell's Angels* and *Journey's End*. Their picture of the carnage and wastage of war appalled him, and many of their scenes are vividly terrible in his mind still. One of his best friends at Margate Central was a boy named Harry Kinlan, a member of Alfred's house and a fellow-member of the football team.* They spent much time together during the summer holidays, bathing, swimming, lying on the sands, or kicking about with a tennis ball. One day they were kicking the ball against the wall of Westbrook Pavilion, pausing from time to time to sit and talk. During one of these interludes Alfred suddenly remarked, 'You know, it's absolutely fantastic, this business of soldiers going out to fight face-to-face. I bet before long there'll be just one man on each side with his finger on a button. All they'll need to do is press the buttons and each other's cities will just be disintegrated.' Startled by this vision, the boys went back to kicking their ball. But the appalling notion never left at least one of them.

The Christ Church Dramatic Society 'enhanced an already good reputation' by presenting J. B. Priestley's *Laburnum Grove*, produced by Alfred Deller, who also played the parts of Bernard Baxley and Sergeant Morris. The local newspaper critic described him in the former rôle as 'mirth-maker in chief'. He went on, 'Looking remarkably like a caricature of Hitler, with a long black lock of hair over his forehead and a small moustache— and wearing loud check plus fours—Alfred Deller was a fit subject for laughter before he had opened his mouth, and some of his lethargic observations were extremely funny.'

Peggy also came in for praise, prophetically enough, as Mrs Radfern, 'whose faith in her husband nothing could shake'.

It was their last stage appearance together. Shortly

---

* To be awarded the George Medal as a fireman in the London blitz.

after, Peggy withdrew from the more arduous social engagements; and on 27 September 1938, just before Neville Chamberlain returned from Munich triumphantly waving his scrap of paper, the Dellers' first child, Mark, was born. In hospital, Peggy had been refused newspapers during the crisis days. Now, with 'peace in our time' seemingly assured, the future seemed to promise unending bliss. Before long, however, a mutual restlessness began to affect the new parents. Peggy recalls, 'I suddenly had the awful feeling that "this was it". Alfred and I seemed to have got all we could expect to have in life, and there was nowhere further for us to go, nothing to aim for. Alfred felt the same. We discussed it, and felt ashamed of ourselves for having almost too much. The thought that his music might be the key to our future never occurred to me, though I think it was constantly in his mind that he would become a professional musician. To me, his music was just his hobby. I had almost ceased to think about it.'

Their gloomy thoughts soon passed under the pressure of new events. With Mark's first birthday less than a month away, war broke out.

As a married man, aged twenty-seven, with a child, Alfred did not immediately qualify for conscription. His work at the shop and his singing at Christ Church continued uninterrupted. For some time the war touched him only lightly. Peggy's mother, sharing a widely held fear that gas attacks were imminent, had gas-proofed one of the large basement rooms of her combined home and business premises. Peggy was pressed to bring Mark to shelter there whenever a siren sounded, and before long Alfred was agreeing to close up their new home and move with the family into permanent quarters in Mrs Lowe's substantial three-storied building.

They had not been there long when he came home from Evensong one day with a copy of the *Church Times*. Ensuring that they were out of her mother's earshot, he explained to Peggy that a bass singer, Percy Sutton, better known to his fellow choristers as 'Laddie', had pointed out to him an advertisement of vacancies for a bass and alto in Canterbury Cathedral choir. Assuring each other that they had little chance of succeeding, they agreed to have a try, subject to family consent. All the way home, Alfred had been thinking not so much of the stiff audition he could expect to face, as the explosion his proposal would touch off in Mrs Lowe's household. Even Peggy might be expected to object. If he were, by some long chance, appointed to Canterbury, it would mean the disruption of their domestic arrangements, and a new threat to their financial security. The pay would be small and it would be necessary for him to find a part-time job, so that he would not have much time to devote to his family. Worst of all loomed the possibility of a row between Peggy and her mother which might have permanent consequences.

To his relief, Peggy raised no objections. If this was what he wanted, then it was what she wanted. The upheaval could be borne somehow. They went to her mother and told her together. Her reaction was surprisingly mild. Without quite saying, 'I told you so!', she merely assured them the whole idea was mad, with no possible future for them. This unexpectedly reasonable opposition caused Alfred a moment of second thought. It was Peggy who determined him. Looking beyond all practical considerations, she saw that it was a thing he must try, or for ever regret. The application went in.

It was not his first shot at a cathedral post. In 1930 he had applied for an alto vacancy at Lincoln, backed by warm commendations from his then present and former vicars at Margate. In spite of the latter's assertion that 'the choir would be fortunate which secured his services', Lincoln declined them. Three years later he had tried for the vacant alto lay clerkship at Salisbury Cathedral, with Hector Shallcross's testimonial to his undoubted gifts. Once again he was disappointed.

Canterbury, with one of the country's oldest choral

traditions, promised to be no easier. Without holding any inflated opinion of his talents, he knew that his voice, with its unusual range over nearly two octaves from G below middle C to G flat, was well capable of all demands it might meet, in solo or in concert. His musicianship had never been criticized. He had full confidence in his ear and instinctive intonation. His choral experience now totalled seventeen unbroken years, more than half of which had been spent in the notable Christ Church choir under the first-rate supervision of Allan Biggs. And— a thing he knew was by no means the case with all professional cathedral choristers—he was a devout Christian and churchman, with an intense feeling for, and understanding of the spiritual function of church music.

Against these assets, he was conscious of one deficiency which, in the eyes of a cathedral Establishment, might nullify them all: he had no formal qualifications. Cathedral appointments tend to be made on a 'closed shop' basis. He had belonged to no Cathedral school, attended no academy; had, in fact, had no tuition at all. Everything he knew he had found out for himself, and everything he could do he had learned as his own teacher. That could condemn him, for a start. His dedicated seriousness of intention was as apparent to himself as to those who had worked with him, but it might not appear so readily at a single interview. His capacity for self-discipline was immense: he could not otherwise have achieved what he had; yet a long dependence on self-discipline, he knew, sometimes made the demands of teamwork hard to accept. Many self-made men, in other spheres than music, had been rejected instinctively by those who saw any individualist as a potential underminer of meek con-formity.

Perhaps the reason why his decision to try for the Canterbury post, with all it would bring in terms of upheaval and dissent, had not caused more rumpus was because it was outside the belief of Mrs Lowe, or Peggy, or even himself, that anything would come of it. But if it should, he told himself, it would represent the fulfilment of a dream he had cherished quietly since his earliest days in the choir of St John the Baptist, Margate. In those days regular Choral Union festivals were still held in Canterbury Cathedral, at which massed choirs assembled from all over Kent took part in a spectacular service. He had gone with the St John's choir, and been overwhelmed by it all: the glory, the shared experience, the massed music in the ancient place of pilgrimage and martyrdom. Later, when he was a little older, he had taken a bus from Margate to Canterbury in order to attend Evensong. He had sat alone this time, listening to the cathedral choir sing the Mendelssohn anthem *O come everyone that thirsteth, O come to the waters.* It had been one of the deepest experiences of his young lifetime. The idea of ever being able to attend the cathedral every day, and occupy one of the choir stalls and sing, had remained his vision of utter bliss.

With such conflicting fears and hopes writhing in his mind, and dressed in his best dark suit, with his gas mask in its little cardboard box looking more absurd than ever slung from his shoulder, Alfred took the train to London to answer a summons to an interview by Dr Gerald Knight, then organist at Canterbury Cathedral, now Director of the Royal School of Church Music. Dr Knight heard him sing and told him that his name would be on the short list. The Precentor, Canon Joseph Poole, now Precentor of Coventry Cathedral, asked him to read a passage from the sermons of John Donne—'These sermons always discover whether a man understands English or not,' says Canon Poole. 'Laddie' Sutton had reached the short list, too, and a few days later they travelled together to Canterbury to sing in the cathedral itself, before the Dean and Chapter. Sutton, who had started it all, was told that he had not been appointed. Alfred Deller carried back to St Leonard's the news that he had been offered the post of alto lay clerk.

for nothing—except her husband. He began to look for a place to rent in Canterbury.

It was the period of the 'phoney war', before the fall of France, and life in Canterbury still moved along more or less normally. All the cathedral services continued to be held, with their usual large congregations. Deller had leisure to savour the supreme delight, of singing the finest examples of English church music in one of the country's greatest cathedrals, although one of his first appearances in his choir stall coincided with an un-spiritual contretemps sufficient to disillusion any novice. The Dean at the time was the late Dr Hewlett Johnson, the celebrated 'Red Dean' of Canterbury, between whom and other senior clergy feelings were, as so often, running high. A leader of the opposition was the late Canon J. M. C. Crum, self-styled as 'God's Protestant' with the function of protecting all that he considered to be in the name of God, Christianity and English churchmanship against the 'Red Dean'. It was Canon Crum's turn of duty as Vice-Dean on the afternoon of Deller's first Evensong. Deller recalls, 'It was two minutes to three, and we stood waiting in that wonderful old Treasury Chapel, with the sun streaking through the windows and everything quiet except for the ticking of the clock. I was almost over-whelmed by the atmosphere of calm and beauty. Then, at a minute to three, the Dean came sailing in, not yet vested, passed between the aisles of the boys and men with a cheerful, "Umm, good afternoon gentlemen, good afternoon boys," and vanished into the Treasury. I noticed that Canon Crum, standing next to me, turned his back on him as he passed. As the clock struck three the Dean called out from the Sacristy, in the friendliest of voices, "Umm, will you carry on, please, Mr Vice-Dean?" There was a moment's pause before Canon Crum shrieked back, "No, I won't!" I stood there petrified, waiting to see what would happen next, conscious of the old Canon next to me white and drawn, absolutely furious. Then, after another minute or two, out sails the Dean, as

52

though nothing in the world has happened, and, "Umm, let us pray." It was an incredible initiation for me into cathedral life.'*

Soon after his brother's arrival in Canterbury, Horace Deller left his employment and went away to work in Bognor Regis with the National Assistance Board, while waiting to be called up into the Royal Air Force. Alfred managed to find lodgings, to which he could at last bring Peggy and Mark, in the house of a woman whose husband was away with the Forces. She had two children and did not care to be left alone. After a difficult farewell to her mother, Peggy and Mark, not yet two years old, made their way to Canterbury. Alfred met them with the news that Court's had given him the sack.

The firm had been forced to lay off staff, and the part-timers were the first to go. The Dellers' weekly income, consequently, slumped to three pounds. It was barely enough to pay their landlady, with hardly anything left over, and before Alfred had time to begin looking for another job a far graver event occurred: France fell, and the remnants of the British Expeditionary Force struggled home through Dunkirk.

At last the fact of war hit Canterbury. Until now there had been air raid warnings and an occasional haphazard bomb from single aircraft. There were next to no anti-aircraft defences. Now, plans for the evacuation of women and children were put into effect. Amongst the first to go were the boarders of the cathedral choir school. With their headmaster, Clive Pare, they were transferred to Par, in Cornwall, where they would function as a school for the rest of the war. And within a few weeks of rejoining Alfred, Peggy was ordered to assemble Mark, one suitcase,

---

* An even more startling initiation would have been at that Evensong at another, nameless, cathedral, which provides one of his most-repeated ecclesiastical anecdotes. A lay clerk who had imbibed unwisely in the earlier part of the afternoon was about to sing a solo. The organ had just finished the introduction when the man changed his mind, turning instead towards the Dean's stall to declare loudly, 'I never did like you, Mr Dean, nor your bloody daughters!'

food to last one day, and no drinks of any kind, and report early one morning to Canterbury railway station.

She found herself amongst a seething crowd of women and children. At nine o'clock evacuation officials herded them into railway carriages and locked the doors. There were no corridors. As they chugged slowly along some roundabout route to an unknown destination, the reason for the ban on liquid refreshments became apparent. For the women and children of her compartment at least, Peggy proved the saviour of the day. With supreme foresight she had given up a bit of her valuable luggage space to pack Mark's 'potty'.

London had been raided severely that day, and the train went by a roundabout route to avoid it. As night fell it entered Oxford. The carriage doors were unlocked and the distressed occupants released. Billets had been arranged for them, but the London raid had sent a flood of evacuees scattering to the closer provincial towns. Many had reached Oxford and had filled the billets before the Canterbury contingent arrived. Harassed officials and voluntary workers herded the exhausted women and crying children into a schoolroom for the night. There was still nothing to drink and the lights could not be put out, so that the children went on milling about and sleep was impossible. Again, Peggy was able to do the trick. She created such a fuss that tea was produced and the lights were put out.

As she tried to sleep she saw the dark shape of someone stooping over her. An official whispered to her to pick up Mark and come with her. Outside they were put into the charge of a policeman and led through the streets to a house. The policeman thundered on the door. It was getting on for midnight. When the householder and his wife appeared the policeman informed them that Peggy and Mark would be lodging with them for six weeks. Then he vanished into the night. No doubt comforted by the thought that they might have had a mother and twelve children thus delivered to their doorstep, the couple welcomed her in. She still believes that the whole thing had been quickly organized by the reception authorities because they could spot a trouble-maker when they saw one.

Back in Canterbury the entire atmosphere had changed. The cathedral organization had changed, too. Dr Knight had been conscripted into the R.A.F. The Precentor, Canon Poole, a fine musician whose duties had hitherto been more concerned with choir discipline and adminis-tration than with the music, had been placed in charge, with the sub-organist, William Harvey. The choir itself was much reduced. There is normally a double choir of boys at Canterbury—twenty-four boarders and twenty-four day boys. With the boarders gone to Cornwall and some of the day boys evacuated there remained a total of five lay clerks and six or seven little boys. Canon Poole had to supply the missing tenor part on the cantoris side, and often had to answer himself in versicles and responses. Gradually local boys came in, and within a couple of years they had twenty-four boys, so that services were main-tained right through those hazardous times.

'We had the time of our lives,' Canon Poole recalls. 'Being on the brink of eternity made it much more fun being here.'

Deller found himself constantly called upon to take over the top line in anthems and help out the boys. It added further to the interest of his work. He was still eager to sample all musical experience, and knew how much more of it still awaited him. He was twenty-eight, but he had still not heard the term 'countertenor'.

A few weeks after his twenty-ninth birthday his call-up papers came.

*

He had abhorred violence from boyhood. Even before the war he had been sufficiently moved by the world news to write and tell his father he felt himself to be a pacifist. The Sergeant had responded in a way characteristic of many men who never pause to doubt their own conception of duty, manliness and courage: he answered that, while he could not approve, he understood. Coming from an uncompromising old soldier, whose haven of contentment was the drill hall and whose reading was the drill manual, the letter moved Alfred very much. Not all people, he was to find, would sympathize so readily.

He had his first unpleasant experience of what pacifism could mean to others when, early in the war, he went to Canterbury Labour Exchange to register for military service. There were young men milling around him, making a lot of noise, and he had to shout to make the clerk hear that he wished to register as a conscientious objector. He was overheard. A chorus of jeers broke out. Violence seemed possible, and he was ushered quickly out of a back door. He was spotted, and followed some way by cat-calling men.

He had never discussed pacifism with Peggy. Broadly she knew his views, and approved of them. He had no illusions about what Hitler and his kind stood for, and fully recognized its evil. At the same time he saw, as he had done all his life, that fighting was evil in itself. He understood the motives of his friends who went willingly to join the forces—but for him these motives were not valid.

What depressed him was the belief that so many of those who submitted to conscription and meekly took up arms were pacifist at heart. At a personal level, every man should know his vocation, whether for peace or for war, and should be unafraid to follow it. Totalitarianism, whether Fascist or Communist in kind, was the supreme example of what he termed 'the disease of Secularism—life lived apart from the worship of God through Jesus Christ', which he believed had brought the world into its present tragic state. But, on the evidence of many of their economic and political practices, the democracies, too, were anything but free of the disease. Mankind could only hope to cure itself by spiritual attitudes; war would spread the germs.

Looking back today, he says, 'That was my attitude, and very pompous it all sounds. But, in its essence, it is still my belief. If I had had to die in the war it would have been my wish to die creatively, by which I mean to die offering no resistance. To die having killed someone myself would have been to die destructively, and I saw every act of destruction as being against the good of mankind. The destruction of Hitler and his movement purged a great deal of evil from the world; unfortunately, though, the evils of what I called Secularism are still with us today. This is the enemy all men should be taking up arms to fight.'

This was his case when he appeared on 4 October 1940 before a tribunal sitting at Bloomsbury County Court in Great Portland Street, London. The combination of his views, his profession of lay clerk at Canterbury Cathedral and his willingness to undertake non-combatant duties convinced the members of his sincerity. He was registered as a conscientious objector and instructed to join the Air Raid Precautions organization or find work on the land.

He had already given some passive support to the war effort. Since Dunkirk he had been giving one night each week as a stretcher-bearer, helping to shift casualties being dispersed through Canterbury. It had brought him into contact with A.R.P. workers, whose duties, it seemed to him at that uneventful stage of the war, involved sitting about in shelters playing darts and cards by the hour. He chose the land.

The problem now was to find a farmer close enough to Canterbury who would take on a conscientious objector, totally unskilled at farm labouring, and give him full freedom to carry on with his cathedral duties. He found the Labour Exchange sympathetic and almost miraculously helpful. At Sturry, only three miles from Canterbury, a Quaker family named Headley were farming. An enquiry brought the reply that they had no vacancy, but would be pleased if Mr Deller would call on them. He went by bus, accompanied by Canon Poole, who knew the Headleys slightly. The elderly couple and their two sons were friendly and sympathetic, but repeated that they had no job to offer. The interview ended and the visitors were invited to step in for 'a simple farmhouse tea'. Disappointed, Deller began to refuse, saying something conventional about not wishing to impose himself. He was surprised to hear Canon Poole murmur, 'Don't be silly, Alfred. Go in and sing for your supper. They're interested in music.'

So they went in and sat down to the 'simple' tea, which proved to be an enormous cold collation, the centre-piece of which was a dish holding the largest number of boiled eggs Deller had ever seen in his life. Then, as now, food was the surest reviver of his spirits. He began to talk, and, as usual, everyone was content to listen to him. In due course, Mr Headley leaned across the table to ask if he would care to sing. Although full of eggs, home-made bread, tea and other luxuries of those days of rationing, he agreed readily.

Canon Poole says, 'I played for him on a not very competent upright piano. I think he sang Purcell's *Music for a while*: at any rate, it was something he did very beautifully. In my opinion, it so captivated Mrs Headley's heart that he was offered a part-time job as a farm hand. If he had not taken a cup of tea on that farm at Sturry that afternoon, the chain of events might never have occurred which led to his becoming recognized as the countertenor of the century.'

Certainly, if the Headleys had not taken him on, he might have had great difficulty in finding any other farm where his situation would be so suited to his carrying on his cathedral duties to the full. Even so, he was in for no soft passage. His wage was to be ninepence an hour. He would have to bicycle to Sturry every morning in time to start work at seven. At nine, he would have to pedal hurriedly back to Canterbury for 9.30 Mattins. After Mattins, back to Sturry for another hour's work before lunch; an hour or two more labouring after lunch, then back to the cathedral for Evensong. On Friday, his free day from the cathedral, he worked at the farm all day, and at especially busy times such as harvesting and threshing he had to be excused from choir duties altogether.

'It was back-breaking when I first started,' he recalls. 'I'd never done such hard physical work before, and then there was the cycling to and fro, always behind time. But before long I was as fit as a flea, and loved it all.'

He wore colourful shirts of red, orange or blue, made up by Peggy from old casement curtains. Outdoor life darkened his skin, which, with his black hair, earned him the reputation amongst the villagers of being a 'bloody eyetalian' prisoner-of-war, and there was some talk of messages being flashed to the enemy by him.

There was no time to change before dashing into the cathedral. His cassock covered his farm clothes, gum boots and all. His nearest squeak was when he tore into the choir stalls with seconds to spare before the start of a special service for the visiting Russian Primate.

'I fell into my stall, barely able to speak. A manuscript part I'd never seen before was thrust into my hand. The words were in anglicised Russian, a chant of welcome, or something. Within a minute of throwing my bicycle down outside I was singing everything from Vladivostock to Smolensk I could think of. Anyway, it worked.'

Peggy, meanwhile, was moving around Oxford. After she had been eight weeks at her first billet, her hosts reminded her that the period for which they had been required to take her had expired a fortnight before. Instead of applying to the appropriate officials, she simply walked down the road to a large house where she knew there were no evacuees, rang the bell and announced that she had arrived. There was a nursery for Mark, and a nanny, whose room Peggy had to share. They stayed for some weeks, until Peggy got word that an uncle and his family had taken a house at Lambourn, Berkshire. After lonely months amongst strangers who resented their presence she was glad to take Mark to live amongst her cousins and their children.

For some time Alfred had been lodging in Canterbury in the home of a fellow lay clerk, Reg Tophill. Now, he moved into closer relationship with a couple with whom he had been developing a friendship since not long after his arrival in the city. Geoffrey Keable was rector of the ancient church of St George the Martyr, in Canterbury, where Christopher Marlowe had been christened in 1564. When he had appointed Keable in 1933, Dr Hewlett Johnson had informed him that since he himself had time only to deal with national affairs it would be up to Keable to 'stir up Canterbury'. This the new rector and his wife, Gladys, had set about doing with a vigour which had promptly brought roars of reactionary wrath dinning in their ears. Charges of Bolshevism, blasphemy and un-British activities were hurled. In fact, what the Keables and an eager group of church members were doing was almost precisely what Alfred Deller and the Christ Church Young Group had been trying to achieve, to bring the church out of its isolation to play a responsible part in the social and political affairs of the world.

With no qualifications, but guided by the celebrated example and teaching of Conrad Noel, Vicar of Thaxted, Essex, the St George's Group, or Canterbury Lambs, as they sometimes called themselves, set out to associate themselves with more progressive movements in the city with the aim of creating a favourable climate of Christian public opinion. Geoffrey Keable gained election to the local unemployment committee. His wife stood three times for the Labour Party at municipal elections, though more for propaganda value than from an expectation of being elected. The many slums still remaining, despite all that had been done by a former Dean, Canon Bell, provided another obvious target. The Quakers, small in number but influential, made it possible for the St George's Group to convene a meeting at which the Canterbury Churches Housing Fellowship was founded to recondition old houses and give constructive advice to the city council. It functioned valuably and successfully for a number of years.

The Group looked beyond the boundaries of Canterbury for objectives. It helped the Peace Council and the Spanish Aid Committee, getting up meetings, displaying posters, distributing literature, collecting money and clothing for refugees. It 'adopted' a Spanish child. One year the St George's Sunday School children shared their Christmas party with Spanish children, the next year with little Austrian Jewish refugees.

They were not essentially pacifists. The question, could Christianity be reconciled with any kind of violence at all, was a frequent theme of their debating sessions. The group's aims were to combat Fascism, to fight every kind of apathy, and, first of all, to drag the Church out of the Precincts and into the streets. They made many mistakes, of both tactics and tact. The more controversy they could provoke, the more publicly-uttered abuse they could attract, the more encouraged they felt to press forward. The mayor and corporation were invited to attend St George's for a civic service on St George's Day. A councillor replied publicly that it would be an affront to the ratepayers for them to accept. Before the war had begun it was already being put about that the St George's Group were working to soften the will of the populace to resist if Germany should ever attack, a strangely illogical charge to level at a visibly anti-Fascist body. There was an even more distasteful rumour that the children of St George's Sunday School were being taught to spit on the crucifix.

Geoffrey Keable, now rector of Barnham, Sussex, says, 'In so many parishes the question is constantly arising, "Is it worth while dividing a congregation, arousing hostility, emptying the pews, losing money?" One must judge for oneself; but it was clear that no new life could have come into St George's without those early reverses. We made many staunch friends, both within and without the boundaries of the parish. Conrad Noel showed us how to look for the working of the Holy Spirit in bodies outside the confines of the church. We found it true that many who thought they had repudiated the teaching and worship of His followers were yet unconsciously carrying out Christ's spirit in their lives. We argued and discussed and worked, afterwards worshipping together in devotions before the Blessed Sacrament. We argued with atheists on the existence of God. We read papers on the social meaning of the Sacrament. We thrashed out the question, Can a Christian be a pacifist? We believed it was blasphemy to pray for peace unless we also did all we could to bring it nearer. St George's worked and prayed in the belief that a live church group must learn about events of our time and use its small powers to help shape them. Looking back, one regrets many mistakes, but chiefly that we were not able to do more. At any rate, when the storm burst in 1939, there were some who were awake and understood.'

The Keables' and St George's most controversial days were over when Alfred Deller got to know them, but the work and beliefs of the energetic young group brought an immediate response from him. Although he 'belonged' to the cathedral, his desire to be associated with an Anglo-Catholic church had brought him to St George's. He paid his first visit to the Keables on Easter Sunday afternoon, 1940, having been warned by someone, 'They're all mad.' He arrived at the rectory in his Sunday suit, a sober pin-stripe. He rang the front door-bell: there was no response. In the distance he could hear laughter and someone playing a recorder. After a suitable pause he rang again: no one appeared. Diffidently, he walked round the house to the garden. A large and eccentric-looking group was huddled around a priestly figure wearing a cassock. A barefoot recorder-player, sitting astride a garden swing, spotted the stranger and called to the priest. 'Ah!' exclaimed Geoffrey Keable, hastening over to him. 'Do have a fig sandwich!' It was the beginning of what Deller regards as six of the happiest and most rewarding years of his life.

He started cautiously, though. 'My first reaction in approaching a church and a priest, both of which I knew were unpopular with the local Establishment, was to keep my guard up. At Christ Church we had been a very small minority group out of a large and fashionable congregation. We had been tolerated because the rector had approved of us. At St George's I found almost the entire congregation involved in this attempt to apply Christianity to economics and politics. I felt I ought to be wary, but it only lasted for a moment. When I met Geoffrey Keable, and saw how his rectory was an open house and centre of the community, it made a tremendous impression on me. I could see that for these people the liturgy was the centre of life and the thing on which all their activities were based. Then there was the intellectual side. Gladys Keable organized the Marlowe Club to read plays and hold discussions. It probably all sounds absolutely hair-raising and arty-crafty, but it wasn't. The local milkman was one of the leading figures. There were some chaps from the railway, some schoolgirls, an architect. Some of the older people were in it, as well as we young ones. Everything we did had something in common with what I felt, and it influenced me immensely.'

The rectory was known to the Group as the 'George and Dragon', and they came and went as they pleased, day or night. 'In those days there were no organizations like the Samaritans or Alcoholics Anonymous, and so forth, so all sorts of people would come to us for help,' Geoffrey Keable explains. 'From time to time there would be an ex-criminal living with us, or a homosexual, or someone just out of a gas-oven or an asylum. They were totally accepted as part of what was in effect a large Christian family.'

Some weeks after Peggy had left Canterbury, Gladys Keable was evacuated to Guildford. Her husband proposed to Deller that they set up a bachelor 'chummery' at the rectory, which they did, with the milkman as third member. It was an hilarious interlude, with two such 'natural buffoons', to quote Mrs Keable, as Alfred Deller and her husband in close proximity. For each of them the endless private jokes, the bandying of Surrealist quips, and Deller's mimicking of the cathedral clergy served as a safety-valve to ease off the pressure of hard work and frustration. Deller was working long hours at two occupations, each of which, in its way, demanded all he had to give. He had also resumed his stretcher-bearing duties one night a week at the Kent and Canterbury Hospital. He found these varied duties satisfyingly worth while, but he was ever conscious that time was slipping away for him. He was nearing thirty, and almost penniless. He had attained a place in a notable choir and was filling it with distinction, an achievement which at one time would have satisfied all his ambition. Now, he was impatient to go further and make an individual name in music. If his chance to do so did not arrive before long it would be too late: he would have no future except that of an ageing cathedral alto.

By now, Peggy was anxious to return to Canterbury. The daily woman who 'did' for the bachelor household at St George's was not altogether satisfactory, and Alfred suggested that Peggy should come and live with them and take over the duties. This was agreed and she and Mark moved in. The job was no sinecure. She never knew in advance whether two people or half a dozen, several of them strangers, would sit down to the next meal. However many there were, the same rations had to suffice. More than once, one small 'Woolton pie'* intended for four or five would finish up feeding a dozen. But she was glad to be back with Alfred, and although large numbers of enemy aircraft could be watched almost nightly passing over Canterbury towards targets further inland there was little to suggest that a woman with a small child and

---

* A wartime concoction of vegetables and pastry, named after the Food Minister, Lord Woolton.

another baby due in a few weeks' time would be safer anywhere else.

31 May 1942 was Alfred Deller's birthday. It was a Saturday. Gladys Keable had just left the rectory after one of her periodic weekend visits from Guildford. Another visitor was Peggy's mother, in Canterbury for the first time and feeling rather out of place in such uninhibited company, but doing her best to live up to the high spirits around her.

It had been a gorgeous day. Alfred had sung at Evensong and then assisted Geoffrey Keable to give a concert of gramophone records to an audience of soldiers. In the afternoon Peggy had taken her mother walking all round St George's parish, with its narrow streets of ancient houses clustered under the towering cathedral.

A few hours later there was no parish left. At one o'clock in the morning of Trinity Sunday, instead of passing Canterbury by as usual, the massed bombers struck.

FIVE

Mrs Lowe, sharing a room with Peggy and Mark, listened apprehensively to the drone of approaching aircraft and roused Peggy, who reassured her that the siren went every night as planes passed over heading for London. Only if 'Tugboat Annie', the hooter which would sound the imminent warning, were heard would they need to do anything.

The planes were nearer. There was no anti-aircraft fire. Mrs Lowe could hear a sort of tinkling noise against the sound of the bombers. When Peggy listened she could hear it, too. At that moment 'Tugboat Annie' began to blare. The door burst open and Alfred came in, crying, 'They're here!' The tinkling sound had been the patter of incendiary bombs raining on the roofs and roads of Canterbury.

The women leaped from their beds, and Peggy grabbed Mark. Seconds after she had lifted him up a fire-bomb plunged through the ceiling and fell in the centre of his cot. Alfred stayed to put it out as the women went downstairs, to sit in a corner of the hallway which seemed to offer most safety. They chose well. Other incendiaries came through the roof and into various rooms, to be dealt with promptly by Alfred and the rector. When the high-explosives began to fall soon afterwards a bomb exploded some twenty-five yards away, demolishing several houses with the force of its shock waves and blowing the rectory door across the hall. The sheltering women and child were untouched. The house next door was in flames; the gas main in the street was burst and flaming; the express-train roar of high-explosive bombs seemed to be heading straight towards them, while incendiaries continued to make the night brilliant. The one member of the household who expected to live through that night was Mark, aged three. At the height of the noise and confusion the little old lady from the burning house next door ran into

66

the rectory, terrified. Mark greeted her, 'Hello, Mrs —!
Will you have a sweetie?' Their fear was never quite so
great after that.

Several hundred aircraft had converged on Canterbury
simultaneously. From 1 a.m., thousands of incendiaries
had been dropped to light the target, starting raging fires
in the town centre, with its mass of ancient, tinder-dry
houses. Bombing with high explosives followed and
continued until 2.15 a.m. The whole historic area of
twenty-four acres from Watling Street to Burgate Street
and from Rose Lane and Butchery Lane to Lower and
Upper Bridge Street was blazing. It would continue to
flare up at intervals for a week. Three-quarters of St
George's Place was burnt out. The historic old church was
gone, except for the tower, which remains today in the
centre of the rebuilt area.

When the 'All Clear' sounded and it was safe to go into
the street, a horrifying spectacle greeted the St George's
household. Flames, sparks and smoke towered into the
sky so thickly that it was impossible to see whether the
cathedral still stood. According to hurrying passers-by it
had been levelled to the ground. There was too much to
be done in the shattered parish of St George's to allow
them time to go and find out the truth. It was not until
next morning, when Alfred cycled to report for duty at
the hospital, often dismounting to carry the bicycle
through piles of smoking debris, that he saw that the
cathedral still stood. It was virtually undamaged. There
had been direct hits on buildings immediately beside it,
including the chapter house, the library, and part of
The King's School. Many incendiaries had fallen on the
cathedral roof, only to be pushed straight off by the long
poles of firefighters stationed there, high above the ground,
thanks in great part to the foresight of the 'Red Dean'.
He had also had the idea of preparing the cathedral crypt
as a safe shelter, capable of holding hundreds of people
from near-by houses. Although St George's parish had
been wiped out in an hour, the loss of life had been

mercifully small, for most of the householders had taken advantage of the cathedral's ancient sanctuary.

When the news reached the Headleys, at Sturry, they sent word at once, insisting that the Keables and Dellers come to the farm to stay. There was nothing left to be done in Canterbury, which swarmed with firemen and salvage workers from places as far away as Woolwich. Mrs Lowe returned home, leaving the three Dellers and Geoffrey Keable to move out to Sturry, where they thankfully settled down for an early night.

During the day, barrage balloons had been rushed into the area and now ringed the city. When the bombers returned that night, few were able to get through. Frustrated, they dropped their bombs on the outlying areas, one of which was Sturry. The rectory refugees found themselves for the second night running in the thick of a combined incendiary and high-explosive raid.

In the space of an hour some 1,500 fire bombs fell on the Headleys' property. One 'Molotov Breadbasket' container full of incendiaries landed squarely on the centre of the roof of the farmhouse, splitting on impact, as it was designed to do, and sending its bombs scattering down the front and back of the building. Incredibly, not a spark touched the roof, but the whole farmyard seemed to be alight. A haystack was flaming like a torch, so brightly that the swastikas on a low-flying bomber's wings were clearly visible by the light. Straw lying about the yard was blazing, cars and equipment were burning with oily smoke and a stench of rubber. Some bombs crashed through the corrugated iron roofing of the pig-sties and the air began to ring with the animals' terrified screams.

Bertram Headley, Geoffrey Keable and Alfred, wearing pyjamas and steel helmets, dashed from the farmhouse towards the sties. Deller remembers, 'Several times we saw planes coming and had to go flat on our faces till they were past. When we reached the sties there was pandemonium. There was one great sow, screaming her head off, with the straw burning all round her. I kicked open the door and she ran out. Just outside the sty was a pile of mangel-wurzels. As soon as she saw them she went straight up and started to eat them, though she'd been terrified nearly to death a moment before. I was scared stiff myself, but I had time to take it in as a reassurance about the extent of animals' feelings of fear or pain.'

Although the damage to the farm had been miraculously slight, there was not accommodation for the Dellers to remain there for any length of time. With her second baby's birth drawing near, Peggy evacuated herself again, this time to Little Chart, near Ashford, where an elderly relation of the Headleys had an ancient house made out of two joined cottages. The old lady was kindly, but impractical. Opening a larder door, Peggy found it full of old and crawling food. She slammed the door shut and never opened it again; but the thought, whenever she passed that way, of what was happening in the larder, together with the general creepiness of a house with two front doors, two back doors and two staircases, so affected her that she panicked. Telephoning her mother that she would rather risk the hit-and-run raids on Hastings, she went home. On 21 October, Simon was born there.

After the birth Peggy returned to live with Alfred and their children at Sturry, where the Headleys had cleaned up and furnished a disused oast cottage for them. The Dellers paid seven and sixpence a week rent, and got it all back in free provisions, including fruit they could pick from their windows. They shared the cottage with innumerable mice which nonchalantly drank from the cat's dish and ran all over baby Simon, with no apparent ill-effects. They were preferable to maggots.

After several months the Dean offered the family the use of the choir school, which had stood empty since the evacuation of its pupils. They moved in with the few oddments of furniture they possessed: it was the first time they had had their own things about them in Kent. It was a comfortable home. In the kitchen was an old Aga cooker, which the Dellers had no idea how to use.

Popping in from the Deanery next door, where he was living, sleeping and working in one small study, the Dean recognized their plight. 'Um, we'll soon get that going,' he said, slipping off his black jacket and kneeling in his gaiters before the fire-door. 'Umm, pass me some wood and paper.'

Deller says, 'A lot of hard things have been said about the late Dr Hewlett Johnson, and I know how disliked he was by many people, both in the Precincts and out in the world at large. I can only say how extraordinarily kind he was to us. He helped in every way he could, from lighting that Aga to insisting that we put Mark and Simon down to sleep in one of the bunks kept for his family in the crypt. Whenever "Tugboat Annie" sounded we would dash over from the choir school to the crypt, and invariably we'd find the Dean there, gaiters and all, organizing things. Whatever time of the day or night it was I never once saw him out of full dress. We thought he must go to bed in his gaiters, because he could never have done up all those buttons in time to get over to the crypt as quickly as that.'

When Geoffrey Keable returned to Canterbury on a visit he found the Dellers moved from the choir school to the warden's house at St Augustine's, the Anglican training college, which was also virtually empty. They lived rent-free in return for Peggy's cooking for the sub-warden. Later, they occupied one enormous room in the college itself, with Peggy's cooker at one end, Alfred's piano at the other, and Mark playing trains in the middle. With his own church destroyed, Geoffrey Keable had taken a curacy at Harrow, refusing to accept another living of his own in order to remain titular rector of St George's and so save the parish from extinction. The bombing had done nothing to destroy the St George's Group, which continued to meet when and where it could: rather, in Geoffrey Keable's words, 'It had bound us together for life.'

It was 'business as usual' at the cathedral, too. 'Like

another celebrated establishment,' says Canon Poole, 'we never closed.'* The bombing had shattered most of the glass, making the main body of the building too exposed for the daily offices to be sung there. The eastern crypt was chosen as an alternative. The very day after the main attack a solemn procession set off from the Treasury towards the crypt, led by the Vice-Dean, old Canon Crum and Canon Poole. As they moved along a side aisle they saw a workman on a high ladder, knocking out fragments of glass remaining in a window. Canon Crum called to him, 'That's right, you do your job and we'll do ours.' They filed on down into the crypt and proceeded to say Mattins, amongst the dust and rubble, with a single candle to light them. Deller found the services in the crypt especially moving. 'The whole thing was alive with emotion. You felt you were in the catacombs, and so much nearer to a full understanding of what Christianity was all about. I think, for me, that was the nearest I have ever come to it.'

Canon Poole was determined that the cathedral music should continue. Sung services were resumed in the crypt, still with a depleted choir of five lay clerks and a dozen or so day boys, with an additional two or three volunteers at weekends. The crypt remained in use as a bomb shelter, and it was while sitting down there one night during an alert that Canon Poole first read the manuscript of a new work he had managed to commission for his small choir. It was Michael Tippett's *Plebs Angelica*.

Poole had developed a keen interest in Tippett's work early in the war since running through blacked-out Canterbury to reach a radio set in time to hear the Second String Quartet. Its affinity with the polyphony of the great age of English music impressed him enough to make him contact the composer, asking him to write a

---

* The proudly advertised boast of the Windmill Theatre, London, which continued its non-stop variety and girlie shows throughout the Blitz and the war.

Mass for Canterbury. Tippett replied that he could not do this, pointing out that as one of the *pagani* he could not sincerely compose a Christian work; and if he were to leave the ranks of the *pagani* he would be abandoning them. 'This was a profoundly Christian statement,' says Canon Poole, 'the statement of a man of integrity and honesty for which I have ever since honoured Michael Tippett.'

To Poole's proposal that he should, at least, write something for him, Tippett suggested that a work much less personally committed than a Mass would be an anthem, and suggested a fragment in honour of St Michael from Helen Waddell's collection of mediaeval Latin lyrics. *Plebs Angelica* was the result, a double-choired motet first performed by the Canterbury choir in the crypt and given its first public performance at Canterbury by the Fleet Street Choir. Deller found it a work of great beauty and interest. He little realized that the commission to the then little-known composer was going to bring about the transformation of his own career.

Tippett was thirty-six. Not many months earlier he had finished serving a three months' prison sentence for refusing to assist the war effort. Now, with his oratorio *A Child of our Time* just performed for the first time, he seemed about to break out of obscurity and achieve a major position in British musical life. Much of his work outside composition had been in the adult educational field. In 1931 he had first become associated with Morley College, London's chief centre for adult education at that time, when its redoubtable principal, Eva Hubback, had engaged him to work with an orchestra of unemployed musicians. Quite early in the war a land-mine had destroyed most of the college, with the exception of the entrance hall, some classrooms and the small music room dedicated to Gustav Holst, the most eminent of the college's musical directors. His successor, who also taught at Westminster School, had left London for good when his pupils had been evacuated, and Mrs Hubback asked Michael Tippett to replace him. It was a labour of love, with scarcely any pay, but an admirable opportunity for a young composer and conductor to get on in his profession. He could work with an already good amateur choir, varying between thirteen and eighty members, which Tippett and his associate, Walter Goehr, improved to the point of excellence. Their free Sunday night concerts became notable in London, attracting crowded audiences of young people, British and foreign servicemen and G.I.s to the various halls in which they appeared. Since before the war, Tippett had been fascinated by the music of Purcell and the Elizabethans. Most recitals by the Morley College Choir included examples of their works, but one difficulty recurred constantly. Purcell had been a countertenor, and he had written for this voice in many of his bigger works. Knowing that there had been no possessor of a countertenor voice for a century and a half in Britain or anywhere else, Tippett had to look for a compromise. Instinct told him that to engage a conventional male alto, out of some choir, perhaps, to sing Purcell would prove anything but successful: as unsatisfying artistically as it would be to use a female contralto

73

for the essentially masculine countertenor part. One experiment he tried was to perform the big *Ode for St Cecilia's Day* with groups of his Morley College singers taking the solo parts in unison. It was partially satisfactory and gained a notice in *The Times* affirming that there could be considerable public interest in such hitherto little-heard works. Tippett saw clearly, though, that the problem of the extinct countertenor stood inexorably in his way.

In the course of their correspondence about the Mass for Canterbury, and the substituted *Plebs Angelica*, Canon Poole had mentioned to Tippett that the cathedral possessed an alto of rare accomplishments and urged him to come and give him a hearing. The opportunity did not offer itself immediately, and the suggestion drifted into the background. It had not been the first time that Joseph Poole had written to established musicians about Alfred Deller. Nothing had ever transpired: having been a cathedral alto, however good, was no recommendation at all in the musical profession's eyes. Scope for the voice as a solo instrument simply did not exist. Deller himself was realist enough to recognize this; and yet he too had for some years been studying, purely for his own interest, the neglected glories of Henry Purcell's work. There had been little chance to do anything practical about it. His many duties kept him far too busy to think of recital engagements, even if, in evacuated and bomb-torn Canterbury, there had been any such opportunities offering. But he had not yet given up hope of some day making a mark of his own in music; and the more he saw of Purcell's music, the likelier it seemed that it could be through this that he would make it.

Once more, Fate lent a hand. At this very moment, when the Purcellian reflections of both Michael Tippett and Alfred Deller had come almost to the point of converging, the two men met. By an extra coincidence it was Gladys Keable who helped to bring them finally together, and that by utter chance.

She had taken the opportunity of a brief holiday in

Cornwall with some other members of the St George's Group, and was now returning by train with one of the girls, Jo Roberts, when a group of men who could only be musicians entered their compartment. In accordance with tradition there was no conversation between the two parties and eventually the train reached Plymouth, where one of the musicians, 'a very interesting-looking person', in Mrs Keable's recollection, got out. The journey was resumed. Again, for all the hours to London no conversation passed. Then, with perhaps half-an-hour to go, Jo began searching for her hat. This broke the ice. All the others helped her search, until the hat was at last unearthed, crushed, from beneath the musicians' luggage. Conversation now flowed freely. What was Mrs Keable reading, the musicians wanted to know? The mediaeval mystics. How interesting! Brief discussion of this topic. Then, from her in return, who had been that interesting-looking man who had got out at Plymouth? Oh, Michael Tippett. Perhaps she mightn't have heard of him, though. Very *avant-garde*. Just out of prison.

Gladys Keable had heard of him, and knew that Joseph Poole had written to him about Alfred Deller. She told them. 'Get him to write again,' advised one of them, and introduced himself as Antony Hopkins.

Joseph Poole did write, and Tippett replied that, as he was coming to Canterbury to hear the Fleet Street Choir give the first public performance of *Plebs Angelica*, he would be pleased to hear the alto sing. In Michael Tippett's own words: 'I was at that time wrapped up not only in Purcell, but in the Elizabethans and all the early English school. One of my heroes was Orlando Gibbons, so the first thrill of that visit to Canterbury was to enter the practice room in the choir school, which I found to be almost unchanged since Gibbons himself was there in the sixteenth century. It was in those evocative surroundings that I heard Alfred Deller sing Purcell's *Music for a while*. It was not a very good arrangement of it; but for me, in that moment the centuries rolled back.'

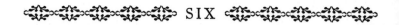

T his was the voice Michael Tippett had only dreamed of ever finding, and which Alfred Deller had only begun to realize he possessed when, studying and singing in Canterbury Cathedral some of the works of William Boyce, he had noticed that his alto part was always designated counter- or contra-tenor.

The question, what is a countertenor?—or when is an alto not an alto?—has been debated again and again without, it seems to the present authors, ever having been answered with definitive clarity. Having broached it, we must not shirk from making the attempt: we suggest that a countertenor is, quite simply, a male alto of exceptional brilliance and flexibility.

When asked to define it himself, Alfred Deller is forthright.

'Two questions have been put to me constantly during my thirty years as a professional singer. The first, which is of a personal, not to say intimate nature, I leave to the imagination. The second is, when did you decide to become a countertenor? This is rather like being asked when I decided to be born. I had no choice in the matter: it just happened. I joined my parish choir at eleven with a good strong voice, a good ear and a good memory. I became solo boy, and by the time I was fourteen had made a local reputation as a soprano. I continued to sing soprano solos in the annual performance of the *Messiah* until I was sixteen. I had no yodelling difficulties during the voice-changing period, and when the organist asked me to continue in the choir as an alto I made no conscious adjustment to my voice production. I couldn't. I only knew the one way to sing. It would have been less embarrassing to have sung a sort of baritone, which I would have been capable of doing, though in an undeveloped and inexpressive way. When, eventually, I met Michael Tippett I was still singing alto and calling myself an alto. He said to me, "When you sing for me, I shall give you the old English classical name for your voice, which is counter-tenor." And that is how I became a countertenor.'

Tippett has defined the voice: 'The countertenor is a male alto of what would be regarded now as exceptional range and facility. It was the voice for which Bach wrote many of the alto solos in the Church cantatas; and Purcell, who himself sang countertenor, gave to it some of his best airs and ensembles. To my ear it has a peculiarly musical sound because almost no emotional irrelevancies distract us from the absolutely pure musical quality of the production. It is like no other sound in music, and few other musical sounds are so intrinsically musical.'

When Tippett revived the term countertenor he was paying tribute to the uniqueness in his time of Alfred Deller. By his great gifts, combining peerless technical facility with consummate artistry, Deller has retrieved the countertenor voice not from extinction, but from eclipse. In the two centuries of that eclipse the tradition of male alto singing has never ceased. It has merely been driven underground—if one may use the term to describe its confinement to the cathedral choir and the barber shop quartet, as opposed to the solo opportunities offered by the theatre and the concert platform. In confirmation of his youthful feeling that, somehow, he was a 'marked man', Deller was to be able to leave the anonymity of the choir stall to fashion a career of his own which would gain him world acclaim. It is no denigration of his gifts, or the way in which he has used them, to suggest that he was fortunate (or 'marked') in the coincidence of several things: Michael Tippett's need for just such a voice as his; the twentieth-century revival of interest in the music of Purcell and his contemporaries, in reaction against the Victorian romantics who played a large part in pushing the countertenor further into obscurity; and the inauguration of the B.B.C. Third Programme, which was to bring Deller, and the countertenor voice, to international notice and admiration.

No alto of Deller's quality had made a mark individually during the past two centuries, and it is unlikely that one has languished unknown. It also seems unlikely that any future alto, calling himself countertenor and making a career as a soloist, will equal Deller's fame. He may be matched some day for artistry and virtuosity; but his place as pioneer is unassailable, and, together with his gifts, assures his uniqueness. Save for a difference in ages—and forty-odd in the sixteenth century was not far from the fifty-plus of today—Thomas Coryate, the English traveller visiting Venice, might have been writing of Deller:

> Of the singers there were three or foure so excellent that I think few or none in Christendome do excell them, especially one, who had such a purenesse and (as I may in a manner say) such a supernaturall voice for sweetnesse, that I think there was never a better singer in all the world, insomuch that he did not onely give the most pleasant contentment that could be imagined, to all the hearers but also did as it were astonish and amaze them. I alwaies thought that he was an Eunuch, which if he had beene, it had taken away some part of my admiration, because they do most commonly sing most passing well; but he was not, therefore it was much the more admirable. Againe it was the more worthy of admiration, because he was a middle-aged man as about forty years old. For nature doth more commonly bestow such a singularitie of voice upon boyes and striplings, than upon men of such yeares. Besides it was farre the most excellent, because it was nothing forced, strained, or affected, but came from him with the greatest facilitie that ever I heard. Truely I think that had a Nightingale beene in the same roome, and contended with him for the superioritie, something perhaps he might excell him, because God hath granted that little birde such a priviledge for the sweetnesse of his voice, as to none other: but I think he could not much. To conclude, I attribute so much to this rare fellow for his singing, that I think the country where he was borne, may be as proude for breeding so singular a person as *Smyrna* was of her *Homer*.

The tribute to there being 'nothing forced' is interesting. *Falsetto* is an unhappy term, as the late Davidson Palmer expressed:* 'The term falsetto is a most misleading one, and its indiscriminate use has been mischievous

---

* In his *Manual of Voice Training* (Joseph Williams—now Galliard, Ltd—London).

in the extreme. The man who invented it has much to answer for. He has caused right to be mistaken for wrong, and wrong to be mistaken for right. He has made what is false appear to be true, and what is true appear to be false. Had it been his supreme desire to do all the injury in his power to the male voice of his succeeding generations, he could not, by the exercise of the utmost ingenuity, have devised means better calculated to accomplish his purpose. Falsetto exists and it should be used.'

For all its name, there is nothing false about falsetto. How can there be? It exists, is produced without artificial aid. The 'singularitie of voice' so admired by Coryate almost certainly owed something to falsetto, as does that of Alfred Deller, who explains:

'There are generally recognized to be two types of countertenor voice. The first, and more usual, is where the fundamental voice is baritone or bass, and the head-voice, or so-called falsetto, is developed to the maximum range. My own voice is of this type. You produce this head voice naturally, and you work on it as you would on any other voice. But, if you wish, you can still sing off the chest, so to speak. Purcell was a countertenor of great ability: he also sang bass in the Chapel Royal choir.

'The other type of countertenor is essentially a high tenor who can either dispense with falsetto entirely, or uses it for the top fourth or fifth of the compass, without perceptible break. Some people say this is the true countertenor; others, that it isn't countertenor at all, but merely a very high, light tenor. Certainly, some singers one hears who are billed as countertenors seem to be just tenors with exceptionally high range.

'All in all, it is a most confused subject, about which a great many vague theories have been propounded. The one thing that is clear is that there is nothing to be ashamed of in using and developing the falsetto extension to one's natural range. I agree with Lili Lehmann, who said, "Most male singers, tenors especially, consider it beneath them, generally indeed unnatural or ridiculous, to use the falsetto which is a part of all male voices. They do not understand how to make use of its assistance and of its proper application they have not the remotest conception.'"*

Much of the modern neglect of falsetto may be due to the cult of the ringing tenor who, in accordance with one of the many dubious conventions of Italian opera, must attack his high notes at full bellow, or be derided for a ninny. Falsetto was valued by earlier generations of Italian singers; even the *castrati* used it to extend their range, and Farinelli's incredible ability to span three octaves certainly owed something to it. One of Pietro Francesco Tosi's observations reads, 'A diligent Master, knowing that a male Soprano, without the Falsetto, is constrained to sing within the narrow Compass of a few Notes, ought not only to endeavour to help him to it, but also to leave no Means untried, so to unite the feigned and the natural Voice, that they may not be distinguished; for if they do not perfectly unite, the Voice will be of diverse Registers.'

The distinction between the 'feigned' falsetto and the 'natural' castrato is a nice one, indeed.

The origins of falsetto are unknown. It is enough to know that men capable of singing falsetto existed in music's earliest days, and could sing with a facility and understanding which boys could not match. A great deal of early music was 'high' in character and included parts for one or more countertenors, of whom there must have been no dearth. Women's voices were not permitted in church music, so that all this considerable amount of music was sung by men and boys. One part they sang was the Discantus, a roving accompaniment to the 'straight' plainsong of the tenor. Another was the Contra-Tenor, lower than Discantus, which wove its way round the tenor, singing 'against' it: the hyphen helps explain its purpose in that role. There were two labels for contra-tenor: Altus and Bassus. In his *A General History of*

* See Appendix.

Music, Dr Burney says, 'In early times of counterpoint, human voices of different compass, occasioned by age, sex, and natural organ, were classed and divided into four distinct kinds, at the distance of only a third above each other, which the Base, or F clef placed from line to line expressed. The lowest of these was called the TENOR, the next CONTRATENOR, MOTETUS the third, and TRIPLUM the highest, or TREBLE, of which term this was the origin.' By the late fifteenth century, under the influence of the

Sistine Chapel, the four parts had resolved themselves further into Cantus, Altus, Tenor and Bassus, the Altus still being known as the Contra-Tenor. In the following century it was de-hyphenated and anglicized into counter-tenor.

The seventeenth century was the countertenor's heyday. It was the heyday, too, of English music, and each owes much to the other. Michael Tippett says, 'I know of nothing comparable whatsoever to the music of the English Restoration. Nothing in any other country's music can surpass, in my view, this great flourishing under Purcell; and Purcell wrote much of it especially for the countertenor voice because history compelled him to. Cromwell had driven choral music out of the church, so that, by the time of the Restoration, there were no boys' voices being trained. Purcell had to train any sopranos he needed. It took him many years to get the tradition flowing again, and it was not until almost the end of his life that he could find boys' voices good enough to achieve the effects he wanted. Meanwhile, he used countertenor, tenor and bass for piece after piece, from the most delicate and intricate to those great odes and massive verse anthems, all calling for a great degree of virtuosity.'

Purcell himself was a better countertenor than most. When he took part in his new ode, *Hail, bright Cecilia*, at its first performance at Stationers' Hall in November, 1692, the correspondent of the *Gentleman's Journal*, doubling as court correspondent and music critic, noted the 'incredible graces' with which he endowed the aria *'Tis Nature's voice*.

During his exile, Charles II had heard some impressive singing in continental chapels: some of it, certainly, by Italian *castrati*, some, perhaps, by Spanish singers trained by the unrecorded and long-lost methods by which many falsettists of great skill are rumoured to have been produced. In 1679, Charles summoned one of the leading English countertenors, John Abel (or Abell), newly sworn a Gentleman Extraordinary of the Chapels Royal, and ordered him to go to Italy, learn all he could, and, it is said, at the same time show the Italians that they did not have the monopoly of good voices. On 24 January 1682, John Evelyn recorded, 'After supper came in the famous treble, Mr Abel, newly returned from Italy. I never heard a more excellent voice, and would have sworn it had been a woman's, it was so high, and so well and skilfully managed.'

Abel may have brought back more than mere hints on better singing. He was receiving worth-while payments of bounty money from the royal purse; not, it is suspected, as a form of bursary, but in payment for his activities as a spy.

When William and Mary succeeded to the throne in 1688 the payments ceased abruptly and Abel was dismissed from the Chapel Royal on suspicion of Romish leanings. He was exiled to the Continent, where he had the resource to travel widely, singing to his own lute. His outstanding voice and whimsical manner made him extremely popular wherever he roamed; except, perhaps, at Warsaw, where he refused to sing before the Court. This situation was soon resolved when Abel was seized, pitched into a chair and suspended over the bear-pit, with the threat that it was a case of sing or be lowered. He said afterwards that he had never sung better in his life.

He was allowed back to England and published a collection of his songs, prefaced by a judiciously worded poem:

> After a twelve years' industry and toil
> Abell at last has reached his native soil.
>
> Not that he vainly boasts of bringing home
> The spoils of France, of Italy and Rome
> Or thinks to please the Judges of the town
> From any other climate than his own,
> But humbly begs since foreigners could raise
> Your admiration and receive your praise.
>
> That he with some advantage may appear
> And bring English pleasure to an English ear.

He was still singing in 1716, when well over sixty, and was said to have some secret means of preserving his voice.

Abel's most celebrated contemporary was Francis Hughs (or Hughes). Burney wrote of him, 'Mr Hughes had been a favourite singer at concerts, and between the acts of plays. For several years he was assigned the part of first man, in the first opera that ever was performed on our stage in the Italian manner. His voice was a countertenor, as we are told in the *dramatis personae* of *Thomyris*; and indeed, as the compass of his songs discovers. He continued to perform the first part till the arrival of Valentini, after which no further mention is made of him either in opera or concert annals.'

A further opera, *Arsinoe*, was produced at Drury Lane on 27 January 1705, with the express intention of introducing singing of the Italian style to the English stage. Thomas Clayton, whose enterprise this was, declared, 'Though the voices are not equal to the Italian, yet I have engaged the best that were to be found in England; and I have not been wanting, to the utmost of my diligence in instructing them.'

Arsinoe proved popular enough, even with its admittedly unremarkable cast, to encourage the production in 1706 at Drury Lane of another opera in the Italian style, *Camilla*. Many of the same singers were engaged, including Hughs. Whether he realized it or not, by appearing in such presentations Hughs was helping to bring about the eclipse of the countertenor. Late in 1707 it was revised, and Hughs once more sang, but this time not as leading man. He had been displaced by Valentini, the alto *castrato*, one of two Italians singing in their own language while the rest of the cast sang English. Valentini's singing, though by no means a great example of the *castrato*'s artificial, yet compelling virtuosity, was enough to set the public appetite astir for more. It was novelty with which no countertenor could compete. Hughs recognized as much, and retired to the uncompetitive haven of the Chapel Royal, where he sang on for another thirty-six years until his death.

Burney wrote the countertenor's epitaph: 'But before a character is given of the great foreign singers who arrived here after the Italian opera was firmly established in this country, it is but justice to say something of the English singers, who were able by their performance to excite curiosity, give pleasure, and set censure at defiance, when the opera was in its infancy, and regarded by some as an idiot, and by others as a shapeless monster.'

As we have seen often enough in our own time, the theatre in England is as susceptible as the rag trade to fashionable change. Music-hall succumbed to revue: musical comedy and light operetta were swept clean from the stage by the glitter and virility of the 'musical'. So it must have been with the coming of the *castrati* at the beginning of the eighteenth century. Nothing like them had been encountered before. Their combination of brashness, flamboyance and mysterious non-sexuality added up to a considerable fascination. Their voices seem to have possessed a bewitching unearthliness. Their virtuosity must have been dazzling.

Their origin is hidden in antiquity. There have always been, and still are, natural eunuchs. Singing beside boys and falsettists they made useful church choristers, being invariably less unruly than the former and generally more accomplished than the latter. They faded from the European scene in the Middle Ages, reappearing again in the fifteenth and sixteenth centuries when papal ears began to tire of the shrill cries of the Spanish soprano falsettists who had established the *a cappella* style, with elaborate and often florid textures beyond the powers of boys and ordinary falsettists. The return of the eunuchs coincided with, and no doubt owed something to, the rise of Italian opera. Opera in the Italian style has been one novelty which has endured, though less on the strength of the works which comprise its repertoire than on the skill and personality of generations of singers who have been content to use the tried and trusted works as vehicles for their own talents and conceits.

Italian opera and the *musici* or *evirati*, as the *castrati* were also widely known, were made for each other. A contemporary wrote, 'Their timbre is as clear and piercing as that of choirboys and much more powerful; they appear to sing an octave above the natural voice of women. Their voices have always something dry and harsh, quite different from the youthful softness of women; but they are brilliant, light, full of sparkle, very loud, and with a very wide range.' Just the thing, in fact, to please Italian audiences; and, it must be admitted, to please audiences wherever in due course they arrived. In Rome and many other places, women were not permitted on the operatic stage until the nineteenth century. They were not much missed with the *castrati* to fill the bill. These exotic creatures, as feminine, often, as any women, and far more accomplished singers, were adored by both the male and female factions in their audiences, off the stage as much as on. Their physical shortcomings (induced during childhood by means of scalding hot baths, to promote near insensibility, and a quick operation with knife or pincers) made them safe playthings for ladies of high fashion, who could afford to dally with them to the limit without fear of an unlooked-for outcome; while gentlemen whose tastes inclined towards their own sex could hope for nothing more voluptuous than a young *castrato* of the type Casanova observed during a visit to Rome in 1762:

> We went to the Aliberti theatre, where the castrato who took the prima donna's role attracted all the town. He was the complaisant favourite, the *mignon*, of Cardinal Borghese, and supped every evening *tête-à-tête* with his Eminence.
>
> In a well-made corset, he had the waist of a nymph, and, what was almost incredible, his breast was in no way inferior, either in form or in beauty, to any woman's; and it was above all by this means that the monster made such ravages. Though one knew the negative nature of this unfortunate, curiosity made one glance at his chest, and an inexpressible charm acted upon one, so that you were madly in love before you realised it. To resist the temptation, or not to feel it, one would have had to be cold and earthbound as a German. When he walked about the stage during the *ritornello* of the aria he was to sing, his step was majestic and at the same time voluptuous; and when he favoured the boxes with his glances, the tender and modest rolling of his black eyes brought a ravishment to the heart. It was obvious that he hoped to inspire the love of those who liked him as a man, and probably would not have done so as a woman.

Another who evidently did not care which sex he attracted had been encountered by Casanova some years earlier in a café:

'An abbé with an attractive face walked in. At the appearance of his hips, I took him for a girl in disguise, and I said so to the abbé Gama; but the latter told me that it was Beppino della Mamana, a famous castrato. The abbé called him over, and told him, laughing, that I had taken him for a girl. The impudent creature, looking fixedly at me, told me that if I liked he would prove that I was right, or that I was wrong.'

No such scandalous propensities marred the character of the greatest *castrato* of all, Carlo Broschi, known always as Farinelli. Farinello is Italian for rogue; yet for all the adoration he earned, both for his singing and his looks, especially from women, he seems to have lived the intrigue-free life of a dedicated artist. He is the only *castrato* known to have been of noble birth. That a nobleman should have allowed his son to be castrated at all is singular in itself. It may have been necessitated by an illness, and the child's father, a bit of a rogue himself by all accounts, perhaps decided to make the most of the misfortune by having his son trained as a singer.

He was sent to Naples when very small to study under Nicolo Porpora, one of the most noted singing-masters and composers of the great age of the *castrati*. The life of an apprentice *castrato* was harshly disciplined, but at the same time sufficiently lacking in supervision to lead to the youth's corruption by predatory men or women. The curriculum was unrelenting, consisting of at least six to eight hours of study a day, including voice-training, deportment, speech, counterpoint, harmony, composition and the playing of an instrument, generally the harpsichord.

Farinelli made his debut in Naples at fifteen, and first appeared in Rome two years later. Burney heard him at this time and illustrated the boy's astonishing powers by retailing the story of a duel:

> During the run of an opera, there was struggle every night between him and a famous player on the trumpet, in a song accompanied by that instrument; this, at first, seemed amicable and merely sportive, till the audience began to interest themselves in the contest, and to take different sides; after severally swelling a note, in which each manifested the power of his lungs, and tried to rival the other in brilliancy and force, they had

both a swell and shake together, by thirds, which was continued so long, while the audience eagerly awaited the event, that both seemed to be exhausted; and, in fact, the trumpeter, wholly spent, gave it up, thinking, however, his antagonist as much tired as himself, and that it would be a drawn battle; when Farinelli, with a smile on his countenance, shewing he had only been sporting with him all the time, broke out all at once in the same breath, with fresh vigour, and not only swelled and shook the note, but ran the most rapid and difficult divisions, and was at last silenced only by the acclamation of the audience. From this period may be dated that superiority which he ever maintained over all his contemporaries.

He continued in this vein for nearly ten years, captivating his audiences by sheer virtuosity and personal charm, until, visiting Vienna for the third time, he was offered some shrewd advice by no less a critic than the Emperor Charles VI. Burney, who had it from Farinelli, recounts:

His Imperial Majesty condescended to tell him one day, with great mildness and affability, that in his singing, he neither *moved* nor *stood still* like any other mortal; all was supernatural. 'Those gigantic strides, [said he]; those never-ending notes and passages [*ces notes qui ne finissent jamais*] only surprise, and it is now time for you to please; you are too lavish of the gifts with which nature has endowed you; if you wish to reach the heart, you must take a more plain and simple road.' These few words brought about an entire change in his manner of singing; from this time he mixed the pathetic with the spirited, the simple with the sublime, and, by these means, delighted as well as astonished every hearer.

This, then, was the complete artist who arrived in England three years later, in 1734. Burney waxed ecstatic:

Every one knows who heard, or has heard of him, what an effect his surprising talents had upon the audience: it was extasy! rapture! enchantment!

In the famous air *Son qual Nave*, which was composed by his brother, the first note he sung was taken with such delicacy, swelled by minute degrees to such an amazing volume, and afterwards diminished in the same manner, that it was applauded for full five minutes. He afterwards set off with such brilliancy and rapidity of execution, that it was difficult for the violins of those days to keep pace with him. In short, he was to all other singers as superior as the famous horse Childers was to all other running-horses; but it was not only in speed, he had now every excellence of every great singer united. In his voice, strength, sweetness, and compass; in his stile, the tender, the grateful, and the rapid. He possessed such powers as never met before, or since, in any one human being; powers that were irresistible, and which must subdue every hearer; the learned and the ignorant, the friend and the foe.

Sir John Hawkins recorded, 'In the city it became a proverbial expression, that those who had not heard Farinelli sing, and Foster* preach, were not qualified to appear in genteel company.'

The most famous tribute of all was the cry of a fashionable lady in one of the singer's audiences, 'One God, one Farinelli!'

The older *castrato* Senesino, so much employed by Handel, was in London at the time. Neither of the two singers had heard the other, and simultaneous appearances kept them from doing so. Then, at last, both were engaged to sing in *Artaserse*, a composite entertainment with music by a number of hands. The spectacle of the two greatest soloists the world had known upon the same stage quite overcame the orchestra at the first rehearsal: they sat gaping at Farinelli's brilliance and forgot to play. By the time the piece was ready for its first public presentation even Senesino was ready to acknowledge his colleague's gifts. Playing the part of a chained captive, Farinelli so melted Senesino that the latter forgot he was the furious tyrant and ran across the stage to embrace his victim rapturously.

The *castrato* craze was at its height, with results often familiar enough since: The *Gentleman's Magazine* observed, 'So engrossing are the *Italians*, and so prejudiced the *English* against their own country, that our Singers are excluded from our very Concerts; *Bertolli* singing at the Castle, and *Senesino* at the Swan, to both their shames be it spoken, who, not content with monstrous salaries at the Opera, stoop so low as to be hired to sing at the Clubs!'

Farinelli spent three years in England, during which

---

* James Foster, D.D., the Baptist, whose vigorous sermons at Paul's Alley, Barbican, and evening lectures at Old Jewry, were regarded by the *beau monde* as the height of fashionable entertainment.

time rival managements frenziedly cashed in for all they were worth on the *castrati*, to the inevitable detriment of operatic standards. He would have stayed on indefinitely if the enterprising Queen Elizabeth of Spain had not thought of inviting him to sing to her husband, Philip V, who had for years been in the grip of melancholia so severe that he could neither attend to his affairs nor take any pleasure in living. Knowing that the King would not consent to hear the singer, the Queen arranged for him to do so as if by accident. It worked perfectly. Farinelli sang in another room; His Majesty 'overheard' him and was captivated. He offered the singer a salary of more than two thousand pounds a year if he would remain at court and give his exclusive services. Farinelli, who must have valued security above the hurly-burly of popular fame, accepted. He may have had other ambitions, such as political power, for he was soon interesting himself in a wide range of matters, from irrigation to horse-breeding, and was listened to at court. He paid for it all by having to sing every night to an audience restricted to the King and Queen and their intimate circle. He told Burney that these recitals invariably had to include the same four songs. After performing them nightly, and no doubt subjecting them to every sort of variation, for ten years, even Farinelli must have exhausted their possibilities. At any rate, they kept him from England.

After a heyday of some sixty years the fashionable interest in the *castrati* waned. Richard Leveridge, a bass who had sung falsetto alto in many English productions of Italian opera, ceased to use his falsetto except to burlesque the Italians. In similar reaction against the effeminacy it had encouraged by so idolizing it, the English musical audience turned in righteous reaction to the massive choruses and virile heroes of Handel, who, since *Deborah* in 1733, had dropped the *castrati* in favour of tenors and basses. He still wrote for an occasional countertenor—for instance, David and Joseph in *Joseph and his Brethren*, 1704—but he was now using *women*, and sometimes in male roles, an ironical example of gynandromorphism.

The *castrati* were gone—before long, they would be gone for good in Italy also. Behind them, the golden glories of seventeenth-century music lay in neglect. The dwindling band of countertenors could look neither to stage nor concert platform for opportunity. There remained the church. But in 1772, visiting Brussels, Burney recorded, 'I was glad to find (at Ste Gudule) among the voices two or three women who . . . proved that female voices might have admission in the church without giving offence or scandal to piety, or even bigotry. If the practice were to become general, it would, in Italy, be a service to mankind, and in the rest of Europe render church-music infinitely more pleasing and perfect.'

Women had found their way into the choirs of Protestant churches in parts of Germany in the time of Bach, who had been rebuked for including his cousin (who became his first wife) and, later, his second wife amongst his singers at Arnstadt and Leipzig. They would soon infiltrate the choirs of Protestant churches in England, though it is only recently that they have penetrated cathedral fastnesses. The hitherto unknown female contralto would make her (to the already-deprived countertenor) sinister appearance. 'Permit me,' wrote a reader of the *Musical World* in 1836, 'to draw your attention to a situation in which myself, and others who have the misfortune of being denominated countertenor singers, are placed by the introduction of female contraltos in most of the festivals and concerts instead of the legitimate altos. For instance, not one of us is engaged at the forthcoming festivals at the Exeter Hall. . . .'

Thus, by approximately the end of the eighteenth century, the countertenor's occupation was all but gone. It is small wonder that, listening to Alfred Deller in Canterbury that day in 1944, Michael Tippett should have felt the centuries roll back.

SEVEN

The centuries having rolled back, Michael Tippett, Canon Poole and Alfred Deller turned to discussing how the long-lost voice of the solo countertenor could best be reintroduced to the musical public. Tippett remembers the conversation well, 'because it developed into a frightful argument between Poole and myself and the deputy organist as to whether I should join the Christian Church. Their view was that, as a member of the church, you were better placed to communicate sympathetically with the public at large. I took a composer's view that, with so many of my fellow men not inside the church, it was a limiting factor. However, when we'd discussed all that at great length, we returned to the question of "launching" Alfred Deller. I wasn't a concert promoter. I only had Morley College, where everything was done on a shoestring, so there was no money available. We decided to make a start by fitting him into one of the Saturday evening chamber concerts in the Holst Room there.'

The concert took place on 21 October 1944. The hall was full, but it only held some two hundred people. The programme included Tippett's own *Plebs Angelica*, a piano sonata by Antony Hopkins, some Bartók and some Handel. Deller took part in two verse anthems, *O sing unto the Lord* by Gibbons, and *My beloved spake* by Purcell, and sang again the solo with which he had so impressed Tippett at Canterbury, Purcell's *Music for a while*, this time in a new version made for him by a recent acquaintance, Walter Bergmann. A lawyer in Germany before the war, Bergmann was one of several talented, foreign-born musicians such as Walter Goehr and Matyas Seiber who had collected around Tippett at Morley College. Others included Norbert Brainin, Peter Schidlof, Siegmund Nissel—three young refugee string players who had been educated in England, and who, with Martin Lovett, became the Amadeus Quartet. As well as the refugees, who worked in factories, there were young English medical rejects, like John Amis and Antony Hopkins, and young women, like Hopkins's wife, Alison Purves. So Morley College music went from strength to strength. Small and large groups of its performers appeared in halls and art galleries in evening and lunchtime concerts. Perhaps the principal single feat of this dedicated collection of professionals and amateurs was to rediscover and record Tallis's 40-part motet *Spem in alium*, composed for eight five-part choirs.

Bergmann was one of this team of enthusiasts; and it is his edition of *Music for a while* that Deller has preferred to use ever since, and has made a sort of signature tune connected with him all over the world. He could scarcely have made a happier choice than this haunting song, with its splendid ground bass, which Sir Jack Westrup* considers, 'apart from Dido's lament, the most satisfying, in technique and expression, that Purcell ever wrote'.

On the last day of the year, at an afternoon concert in the Friends' House, Euston Road, where an audience of more than a thousand could be accommodated, Deller made his true debut. The occasion was promoted to raise funds for the Morley College concerts. Tippett conducted. The programme comprised Buxtehude's *In dulci jubilo*, the Bach *Magnificat*, *Plebs Angelica*, and Purcell's *Ode for St Cecilia's Day*, 1692, the last and greatest of the four odes in which Purcell had displayed the instruments of music contending in turn for Cecilia's favour. Deller's singing, especially in the florid, Italian-style recitative *'Tis Nature's Voice*, which Purcell himself had sung with such 'incredible graces' at its first performance, was a revelation.

In Walter Bergmann's words, 'Suddenly, there was Purcell again.'

It was true. Purcell, the greatest glory of English

---

* In *Purcell* by J. A. Westrup (Dent, London, 1937).

music, had never suffered the complete eclipse of the countertenor voice upon which so many of his works depended for satisfactory performance: even with this subtracted, more than enough remained. Yet, in common with most other composers of his time and before, very little of him had been left visible above the flood waters of that Romanticism which had so exactly suited the taste of the long Victorian age and nearly half of the following century. The first stirrings of revival had come in 1876, when the Purcell Society had been founded with the intention of publishing a definitive edition of his works, the majority of which still only existed in manuscript. A handful of specialists and enthusiasts, aware of the riches they alone could appreciate, had worked on quietly into the twentieth century, against the day when, as it must, fashion would swing. But mere fashion could not set a full-scale Purcell revival going. Unlike his colleagues in letters and art, the composer can rarely communicate directly with his public in his lifetime, and certainly not at all after his death. He must await the arrival of a sympathetic interpreter of persuasive enough gifts.

Lionel Tertis raised the viola from an orchestral instrument of the second rank to a solo one of the first. Segovia brought the guitar from the *flamenco* cave to the classical concert platform. Kathleen Ferrier gave new standing to the contralto voice, and Maria Callas and Joan Sutherland a new look to the worn operatic repertoire.

It would be excessive to suggest that, in his almost unwitting rescue from oblivion of a voice-type which he had scarcely known he possessed, Alfred Deller single-handedly resuscitated Purcell also. It would not be fair to the Purcell Society, to Michael Tippett, nor to several other contributors to the Purcell revival. One of them, Anthony Lewis, Principal of the Royal Academy of Music, who has been responsible for arranging and conducting many notable Purcell works which had seldom been performed since the composer's day, has given his assessment of Deller's part in the revival:

'He has helped to open up a great repertoire of Purcell and Handel, not unknown perhaps to a specialized musical public, but not hitherto accessible in really professional presentation. That is to say, the obstacle in the way of performing those works requiring a virtuoso countertenor has been so great that allowances have had to be made, compromises met, and this has had an adverse effect on the whole status of the performance. Concert promoters, conductors and others with first-class standards to keep up steered clear of these works because they knew that there would be occasions during the performance when the standard would inevitably drop, due to the incompetence of the available alto soloist (or, worse still, female contralto substitute); and so the works never reached the most important platforms.

'Alfred Deller, by his first-class interpretation and unassailable technique, gave such promoters confidence to put on these works at the highest artistic level, bringing them off before a highly sophisticated and critical public. So, quite a number of works which had simply been regarded as historical relics, not normally accessible in the concert hall, came forward into the ranks of the acknowledged masterpieces.'

Deller assisted the Purcell revival, and the Purcell revival helped Deller. Perhaps the starting-point of the new momentum each gave to the other was the concert at Friends' House, though the brief notice in next day's *Times* did not mention him, singling out only Margaret Ritchie and Peter Pears for having sung 'confidently', while 'Not all the five solo voices in the Bach could be said to have reached the necessary standard.' The notice conceded in a back-handed way that 'on balance, a true enough idea was given of certain pages of incomparable music to explain the enthusiasm of a large audience'.

The enthusiasm, at least, was undeniable, even by *The Times* critic. It was reaffirmed at several further concerts presented by Tippett and the singers and musicians of Morley College, at all of which Deller was invited to perform. One of the most important, from the point of view of the discerning type of audience it would be sure to attract, was at the National Gallery, one of the celebrated series which had done so much to keep English music-making alive during the war. Tippett had only one misgiving: there would perhaps be not half a dozen people in the audience who had ever heard a countertenor voice. The rest were in for something of a shock. There might be audible reaction enough to put the obviously nervous Deller out of his stride and ruin this chance of making a telling impression. 'I decided to address the audience,' Tippett recalls. 'I told them that I was very pleased to present Alfred Deller, the possessor of this remarkable countertenor voice, and that I was pleased to hear from him that he was already training his two sons to sing, too. It seemed to do the trick. There were no murmurs when he started to sing, and he proved a great success.'

During this period he was enabled to reach an audience many times greater than the total of those who had heard him so far by being asked to broadcast. He entered broadcasting with a smoothness most artists would envy. There was no audition, no apprenticeship of brief recitals at unlikely hours of the morning. He was engaged straight away to sing the principal countertenor part (billed as alto) in a studio performance of *Hail, Bright Cecilia*, conducted by Constant Lambert. Other broadcasts followed in the B.B.C.'s domestic and overseas services.

Meanwhile, his work as a lay clerk at Canterbury went on. His concert appearances and broadcasts had to be fitted into the time off he could get from this and his work at the farm until released. He did not resent it. He had known throughout his time on the farm that, hard though he was having to work, others were suffering infinitely more than he. He says:

'My conscience never wavered, but my resolution did,

especially during the time of the London blitz. I felt that I wasn't sharing enough in the general suffering, so I wrote to the Church Army, offering myself for duty at one of the refreshment stalls or reception centres they were running in the heart of London all through the worst of the bombing. They answered that there was no opening for me, but at least I felt some relief at having tried to do something more. When Canterbury was blitzed, and we found ourselves in the thick of danger at last, it was a sort of personal relief for me, terrible though it was.

'My conscience was never anything but clear about what I was doing. I was working as hard as I could at a useful job—two useful jobs. My family life was as disorganized as anyone's. I was living from pillar to post, and certainly making no money by remaining a civilian. Yet there would always be moments throughout the war when I would think, "By golly, those chaps in the Forces are making the real sacrifice." It was very comforting, though, to find that almost everyone I came into contact with was sympathetic to my position. There were a few unpleasant incidents. I received an anonymous letter, containing a white feather; and there were some cards—anonymous, of course. I still have one of them. It reads: *"Conchie Deller, Sturry. You are a coward, but you endanger your wife's life."* There were one or two comments from acquaintances, during my first year as a conscientious objector, and a bit of ill-feeling within the family. But then it came round to harvest time on the farm. There were not enough of us to manage the work, and there was no casual labour to be had, so troops were sent to help us. They all knew they were coming to a Quaker farm, and that "conchies" would be around. I worked with those soldiers on the threshing machine, carried away stooks with them, and so forth, and made no bones about my position when we got talking. The heartening thing was that not only did they understand my point of view, but they seemed to share it. It seemed to me that most of them were pacifists at heart, as I believe most men are throughout the world today.'

Between the surrender of Japan, in August 1945, and his release from the farm in the following summer, Alfred, Peggy, Mark and Simon Deller managed to live together in Canterbury and enjoyed the first unbroken period of family life they had known since the beginning of the war. They were able to move from their one room in St Augustine's to a flat in a gracious Queen Anne house near by in Lady Wootton's Green, though Peggy found herself once more in surroundings with a touch of the macabre. The Dellers occupied the two top floors of the house. The ground-floor residents were twenty-five cats, many of them deformed. The owner of the house, a maiden lady, lived elsewhere and visited the house twice a day to feed the strays she had taken in. Otherwise, the animals lived quite alone, and the Dellers kept their doors firmly shut. It was, all the same, a house of great charm and attraction, which Peggy would have loved to have been able to buy and move into permanently. She and Alfred loved Canterbury. They had many friends. Wartime restrictions were beginning to lift and life was becoming at last more relaxed and enjoyable. Deller's occasional broadcasts and concerts were bringing in some extra money. He was doing a little music-teaching in Canterbury schools, while Peggy was also managing to earn a little by working two evenings a week as secretary to the headmaster of the cathedral choir school. Then Deller's Fates decided the time had come for another phase in his life to begin.

He was cycling to the farm one morning when he met the postman, who gave him an envelope imprinted 'British Broadcasting Corporation'. Deller opened it, and went straight back home to show Peggy the invitation to him to sing in the inaugural concert of the B.B.C. Third Programme on 29 September 1946.

The sender of the invitation was Anthony Lewis, then a member of the B.B.C. Music Department charged with arranging the Third Programme's first concert plans. He remembers:

'I first heard of Alfred Deller through Sir Steuart Wilson, who was Music Director of the Arts Council at the time. He knew I was hoping to include some of the big Purcell works in my arrangements, and wondering how I should get over the countertenor problem, and he came to tell me of a very remarkable countertenor he had heard at Canterbury. I managed to hear Alfred, and knew at once that it would, after all, be possible for me to put in Purcell's ode *Come, Ye Sons of Art* as one of the two major choral works in the inaugural concert. The work was hardly known, and, if Alfred had not come along, would probably have remained so.'

It was conducted by Sir Adrian Boult. Benjamin Britten had written a specially commissioned Festival Overture. There was Handel's *Music for the Royal Fireworks*, Vaughan Williams's *Serenade to Music*, Parry's *Ode on a Solemn Music*, and Arthur Bliss's *Music for Strings*, conducted by himself. Lewis continues, 'It was a fine concert of fine music, but its most remarkable feature was the Purcell ode. Alfred sang the first countertenor part, and Lambert Wilkinson the second. The effect of two artists who possessed such unexpected voices singing the duet *Sound the Trumpet* was simply sensational. It was a specially invited audience of the select musical public and all the critics, and there is no doubt that the impact of Alfred's extraordinary vocal quality and personal technique on them made that concert one of the turning-points in his career.'

The sensation is not reflected in the restrained notice from *The Times*, and neither Deller nor his fellow counter-tenor was mentioned by name, though there was some near-praise for them:

'Handel's "Music for the Royal Fireworks" followed. Purcell's ode *Come, Ye Sons of Art* was too alike in scoring for it immediately to assert its individuality, though this little impediment was soon swept away on the entry of

99

the voices, which included two countertenors. It was a revelation to hear the familiar duet "Sound the Trumpet" sung by voices of this unfamiliar timbre, for Purcell obviously intended the resemblance to trumpet tone to have the effect of happy allusion.'

Others made no bones about their enthusiasm. Concert offers began to trickle in. There was tentative talk of some recording. The B.B.C. offered more Third Programme broadcasts. The advent of the Third Programme, the first broadcasting service in the world to consist of a cultural content unfettered by the limitations of fixed timing or the need to compromise with the needs of a mass audience, had been awaited with as much interest abroad, especially in Europe and America, as at home. Deller's distinctive part in the impressive inaugural concert brought him at once to the attention of, literally, the musical world. It could only be a matter of time, dependent largely on the period it would take to sort out the cultural chaos left by the war, before he must be invited to perform in other countries.

Almost at their first meeting, Walter Bergmann had offered him two realistic pieces of advice. The first, intended to preserve his uniqueness and make himself less vulnerable to criticism arising from his choice of repertoire during the time it would take him to become established and independent, was to sing only music composed for the countertenor voice. The second, and less arguable, was to leave Canterbury as soon as possible for London, the essential base for his professional career. This latter counsel had been discussed by Alfred and Peggy, without so far being acted upon. Both were reluctant to give up the only real security they had yet achieved for another leap into the unknown and very likely hostile life of London. Now, however, the move was inescapable, if Alfred were to pursue the promise of celebrity. The Canterbury choir was small, and offered no chance of his employing a deputy to stand in for him while he fulfilled another engagement. He was getting all the

time off that could be permitted, but needed much more. He would have to make a move, and to London. But where? As usual, the question was promptly settled for him. He applied for, and was offered, a place at Windsor, but there was no house available. Instead, he joined the choir of St Paul's.

The advantages would be considerable, as Bergmann, Tippett and all his other professional associates assured him. The choir of St Paul's Cathedral is the country's biggest, with eighteen vicars choral on the full strength,* divided into six countertenors, six tenors and six basses; and thirty-two boys. Deller recalled what Sir Steuart Wilson had once told him: 'The great advantage of being at St Paul's is that you never need be there.' There was much truth in it. The Anglican Church, in one of its more realistic attitudes, does not insist that its professional choristers be fervent, or even practising churchmen, a

---

* Westminster Abbey, the only comparable foundation, has twelve vicars choral.

view which has brought only gain to Anglican church music. Many notable concert soloists have passed through the choir of St Paul's, helping to maintain its notable standard, adding an effective dimension to the offices of worship. At the same time they have justifiably lost no chance to further their secular careers. Consequently, a splendid substitution system had long existed when Deller joined. At Sunday services, except for five free days each year, all eighteen vicars choral were required to be present. On weekdays, only twelve were needed, allowing each man two completely free days. If a man was not free on a certain day when some outside engagement was offered him he could ask one of his free colleagues to stand in for him, and pay him for doing so. In addition, there was a list of 'authorized gentlemen', several of each type of voice, approved by the organist, who could be called upon by a vicar choral to take his place on up to forty occasions each year.

This excellent system promised to benefit Deller more than any of his colleagues. Tenors and basses were in much greater demand for concert work than counter-tenors, and even so liberal a deputy system was sometimes strained by a rush of demands upon it. Of the six counter-tenors, it transpired, Alfred Deller was by far the most in demand for outside engagements, and seldom found himself asked to deputize for one of the others; while they, asked to take his place, were happy enough to accept his payment for doing so. It was, and is, an excellent system of musical patronage, benefiting both church and secular music and helping many professional singers to advance their personal careers. Without it, Deller's own career might have been retarded by several important years, and perhaps prevented altogether from reaching its heights. The St Paul's offer came at precisely the moment it was needed, enabling him to move to London without sacrificing the continuity of his choral work and the small, but regular income it provided, while at the same time giving him the freedom to accept almost every outside engagement which came his way and to catch the chance of success and fame on the wing before the helpful novelty value of his voice could pass.

Grateful as he was for the appointment, the cathedral, through its Precentor, George Sage, a former Canterbury colleague, was delighted to be able to add him to its establishment. The Dellers, who had no capital with which to finance yet another change of home, were given a mortgage by the cathedral and luckily discovered that an uncle of Peggy's was about to move out of his house in Merton Park, Surrey, and would sell it to them. By buying directly from him they were able to save money on middlemen, so that the upheaval, if painful, was not ruinous.

Peggy disliked the new house, loathed making the move, and was worried about the effect on Mark's education. He had been about to start attending Canterbury Choir School as a day boy. When Deller mentioned this at St Paul's he was given the assurance that Mark would be taken into the choir school there instead. The last difficulty seemed to be resolved, and plans were made for the actual move to Merton. Then, a few days after they had arrived in their new home, they learned what no one had thought to tell them before, that Mark's entry into St Paul's Choir School would depend upon a voice and educational test. This was annoying, but not alarming, for Mark, whose voice was already promising, had passed his tests for Canterbury successfully. To his and his family's dismay, the St Paul's examiners declared that he had no voice at all, and refused him admission.

It was the sort of challenge to which Peggy could, and can, be guaranteed to rise. Returning to Canterbury, she saw the choir school headmaster, for whom she had worked as part-time secretary, and told him of their determination that Mark should have the musical upbringing for which he had proved himself fitted. Mr Pare sympathized, but pointed out that he had not managed to win a boarder's place, only a day boy's. Peggy asked if Mark could still attend as a day boy, if she could somehow arrange it. This was readily agreed, and she set off on a round of day boys' parents, seeking someone who would take the responsibility of accepting a seven-year-old boy as a paying guest. It was no easy quest, but eventually a Mrs Newnes agreed. Having won two rounds, Peggy still had one to fight. The choir school fees, plus the extra cost of board, were quite beyond their means, even anticipating a steady trickle of concert and broadcasting fees. She took a train to Hastings and went to see her mother.

'Look, Mother,' she said, 'if we find we can't pay Mark's school bill when it comes, will you guarantee us for a year while I go out and get a job to raise the money?'

Her mother agreed, but her help was never needed. Peggy went back to London and was able to find a job with the Town and Country Planning Association. It did more than save the financial situation: it renewed one of the Dellers' warmest friendships, for the woman who got her the job, and worked beside her, was Gladys Keable.

Mrs Keable recalls, 'They were pretty poor. Mark was eight and Simon was four. Having fixed up the one in digs Peggy had to pay housekeepers and neighbours and people to look after the other while she was at work. After a while she had to go away and organize Town and Country Planning conferences all over Britain, which made everything even more difficult. But I don't think she ever wavered. Alfred's life was his music, and that was how it was going to be. She was getting very little out of it herself. Music was not the whole of life to her, as it was to Alfred. She wasn't wrapped up in it, and I don't think she was happy in the completely strange circle of people Alfred's work had taken them into. She couldn't share his success, either financially or by being able to be with him; and yet I'm sure he owes a great measure of that success to what she has done for him behind the scenes.'

The Archbishop of Canterbury, Dr Fisher (now Lord Fisher of Lambeth) was present at Alfred Deller's last

Evensong. When it was over he took him aside and wished him well. The Dean followed suit, then the organist and choir. As he left the cathedral, Deller broke down. The most rewarding years of his life were over. He was going forward to a place where he knew he was more than welcome, and where it would be his privilege and pleasure to sing in one of the country's finest choirs. From the way things were going, it should be only a matter of time before his name would mean a good deal, far beyond the limited territories in which he had so far moved. Yet, he sensed, nothing in his life would ever be again so cosily ordered, so intimately bound to the family and friends nearest to him. He might become famous, and make money and have things he had never been able to contemplate before; but he knew what it would cost him. He did not think of turning back. At thirty-seven he felt as much a 'marked man' as he had done at seventeen.

On the first day of 1947 he sang for the first time in St Paul's Cathedral.

EIGHT

Mary Deller died that year, in Canterbury Hospital, of cancer of the stomach. She was seventy-four.

With the coming of a second world war, the Sergeant's physical training practice had crumbled away irretrievably. It had taken him most of the years of peace to build it into something approaching prosperity. The splitting up of the family, with seven children leaving home one by one, had eased things by stages. The Sergeant had lost none of his energy with increasing years. His schools retained him year after year, businessmen of increasing sleekness and rotundity came to him for trimming down, children needing postural and remedial treatment were sent to him. The exercises he taught worked wonders with people—Paul Robeson's son amongst them—with asthma and other breathing disorders. He taught Baroness Orczy to fence (she was in her fifties at the time, and already famous as the author of *The Scarlet Pimpernel*, so presumably she did it for the exercise, rather than in pursuit of useful knowledge). The Deller household could afford to have everything delivered to it, and to pay the tradesmen by monthly cheque. The Sergeant gardened as hard as ever, though now for the love of it: he no longer swept the chimneys. Then a second war came and snatched away all they had achieved.

Once more, the old soldier could hope for no active military calling. Like any other civilian of no essential occupation on the Kent coast he had to pack up his things and go to an area where the brunt of the expected invasion could not fall. Regretfully, he took down from the parlour wall the plate with the coloured picture of Lord Roberts, the photograph of himself and his horse in India, the framed chocolate box which had been Queen Victoria's Christmas present to the lads in South Africa. When the last of their family had left them, he and Mary, with great good sense, had made a complete break with the past, turning out all their old furnishings and starting afresh with new. The old war relics had stayed, though; and now, with no capital and their whole income gone at a stroke, the old couple were back to where they had been twice before, in their first days and again after the first war.

They took rooms in London. Deeply concerned for their safety, Alfred kept trying to persuade them to leave. They would not. The Sergeant had picked up a connection with a school and was earning a little. Then their two-roomed lodging received a direct hit. Alfred, who had been pulling any strings he could get hold of, hurried to London and brought them down to Harbledown, the ancient hamlet just outside Canterbury where Chaucer's last tale is told, and Lanfranc's leper hospital, founded 850 years ago, has become a cluster of almshouses round an astonishing Norman church. It was not easy to persuade the Sergeant to accept the almshouse Alfred's influence had obtained. His greatest fear was to lose his independence or rely on the charity of others, in which category he included any form of State assistance. But Alfred's persistence won and the Sergeant and Mary settled into their last and most charming home, with its pretty lattice windows and the big hedge for the Sergeant to clip as meticulously as he still trimmed his moustache. Looking from the window one winter's morning, after it had snowed all night, Mary saw the mantled tombstones, all round in the churchyard, and exclaimed, 'Why, they're like choirboys with their surplices on!' They accepted retirement and settled contentedly into a Darby and Joan eventide—though when victory was announced, it was Sergeant Deller, never mind his seventies, who went up the long disused steps of the belfry which had stood since before Magna Carta and got the Union Jack hoisted at the top.

But now, after fifty years of marriage, Mary was gone. She took the fierce old man's spirit with her, leaving him bewildered and lost. For all his well-intentioned tyranny, she had been the one who had really run things. In her quiet, accepting way she had been the mainstay, support and comfort of them all, the Sergeant included. In their last years together she had become the dominant one.

Though he had never realized it, none of them would miss her more than he. Left alone, still active but with all occupation gone, and denied by life-long habit the solace of reading, he was a sitting target for the senile decay which proceeded gradually to overwhelm him. His remaining five years were ones of sad decline, but Alfred Deller retains one memorable impression from almost the very end, in 1951. Visiting his father in a nursing home at Westgate-on-Sea, he sat waiting for one of the brief spells of lucidity in which the old man would recognize him and be able to exchange a few sentences before lapsing once more into meaningless rambling. Suddenly, the Sergeant burst into song. It was his old favourite, *Swing me up a little bit higher*. To his son's astonishment, the voice was a tenor of lovely, true quality. 'I'd never heard him sing like that before,' he recalls. 'His eyes were shining, and he sat, propped up with a pillow, and sang the old song, remembering every word, in this astonishing voice. That was the last time I saw him. He was buried near my mother, at Margate.'

Following the brief, sad family reunion occasioned by Mary's funeral, Alfred returned to London and the steady progress of his career. He had settled quickly into the new routine of St Paul's and was already receiving proof of its benefits to his concert career. He was now being asked to sing at festivals and performances far from London and to broadcast frequently. But if he took advantage of every chance his cathedral post gave him to further his own ends, he gave plenty in return. His influence on church music, both in performance and in repertoire, has been considerable.

'He has exposed the poverty of the cathedral alto, and persuaded people in charge of cathedral music to work to get more musical and more agreeable sounds in the alto line,' affirms Canon Poole. 'I don't think even King's College, Cambridge, would have gone so far as to produce that perfect blending of the altos with the tenors and basses but for the example of Alfred Deller's voice. His influence on the repertoire has probably been more oblique. By playing such a part in the revival of the music of Purcell and the Golden Age through the medium of the Third Programme, he helped to shame cathedral organists into purging their repertoire of much music which, when looked at alongside such masterpieces, had been shown up as valueless. None of us realized just how valueless, until we got another standard of comparison, which Deller helped to bring us.'

'Until Deller, the alto was regarded as a sort of vice that one had to put up with,' Sir Jack Westrup adds. 'Many cathedral organists have groaned under the burden of their altos, particularly altos who grew old and did not become more pleasant with their age.' Had women been admitted to cathedral choirs, it is possible that there would have been no alto revival for Alfred Deller to lead. Altos have kept their place not because of, but in spite of themselves; not because of their artistic value, but by tradition. His example has given incentive to more boys to develop a gift for an alto voice through into manhood, instead of shamefacedly letting it drop. No other countertenor of his stature has emerged as a result; but there is no doubt that the increased number of those who today sing countertenor in the concert hall, or alto in the cathedral, sing better because of him.

In 1948 he made yet another firm friend when Canon L. John Collins joined St Paul's as Chancellor. Canon Collins ('I was not quite so busy in those days as I am now') made a practice when in residence of joining the organist and some of the choir for coffee after services. Before long Deller and he had recognized much of themselves in each other and were taking their coffee tête-à-tête. He recalls, 'We used to talk a lot of rather critical stuff about the cathedral singing. As Chancellor I had to do with the choir school, but not with the choir as such. Later I became Precentor and got to know much more of Alfred's musical views. They were very definite ones and we spent a lot of time discussing ways of improving the services. In fact, I always used to discuss things with him before I made suggestions to the music authorities, so that I could talk with some measure of musical authority myself. Many of the improvements that were made sprang originally from him. For instance, in services when we only had men singing, the practice had been to share alternate verses of the psalms between the choir and the bass soloist. It meant that if you happened to have your weakest bass on duty you were stuck with him as soloist. Alfred got me to have that altered, so that the verses were sung antiphonally, between the two sides of the choir. It was his idea to stop having the Amens played on the organ, and to start using settings by Byrd, Morley, Tomkins and others in addition to the eternal Ferial and Tallis for the versicles on saints' days. The outcome was that the services became much more musically agreeable, and at the same time more devotionally fitting. He impressed me as having a strong instinct for what was most appropriate. I put it down to his being not only a good churchman, but a Christian who understood deeply that his Christianity had to be worked out in everything he did in his life.'

If there is a single master key to any man's character, this is the one to Alfred Deller's, as, indeed, it is to Canon Collins's own. Another who shares Deller's instinct for action through Christianity and, with her husband, helped him to develop and express it, is Gladys Keable. 'Essentially, I think he still finds that the faith he had been taught when he was young remains acceptable and valid for him, and he continues to base his life on it,' she says. 'He has a tremendous sense of the wholeness of life; that the whole experience is not one to be divided into separate compartments of religion, music, pacifism, politics, or anything else. In bringing out the whole beauty of music he is bringing out something that is a beautiful part of life, and of the Trinity; and so he does it as perfectly as he can, as an act of worship.'

It is a creed which leaves little room for compromise; and only the great artists and individualists can occupy their vulnerable position without compromising in some way. Though he had his moments of doubt, Deller did not shirk to act out his pacifism to the full in wartime. Nor has he failed since to hold to his artistic beliefs in the face of all criticism. His voice, he well knows, is not to everyone's taste. There is nothing he can do, or would wish to do, about that. Certain liberties of rhythm and phrasing which he insists upon taking, and one or two platform mannerisms—'Dellerisms', they have come to be called—provoke varying degrees of annoyance in some of his hearers. The knowledge of this does not perturb him. There are few who have been associated with him, professionally or privately, who have not been able to regard his foibles as marks of his uniqueness, or, at worst, as amusing eccentricities; and almost every one of his critics has acknowledged his achievement and stature. More as man than as artist, he sees himself as imperfect in many ways; yet the few real hostilities he has encountered have, at the time, outweighed all else and depressed him deeply. He is unable to remind himself that he is being criticized merely for some detail of performance, not for some personal shortcoming. It is as Alfred Deller, artist, man and Christian all at once, that he has incurred displeasure; and suggestion of failure in any single respect implies for him disapproval of the whole. For a brief moment, it undermines the foundations of his being.

Such criticism, however, was almost unknown to him at this time in the late 1940s when his career was still young and vigorously budding. His worries then were more tangible ones. Money was still very scarce. As well as the two boys, whose boarding-school education had to

be paid for, there was now baby Jane. Freelancing, an insecure enough state in any profession, taxes hardest those who have come up from little or nothing: they know too well what awaits them at the bottom again. The spectre of financial calamity has never been far from Alfred Deller's thoughts.

An invitation, which seemed to have been long in coming, to make a gramophone record for His Master's Voice proved to be unrewarding financially but immensely valuable in other ways. He sang *Music for a while* and *If music be the food of love*, both by Purcell in editions by Walter Bergmann, who accompanied him on the harpsichord. The disc caused a discernible stir in musical circles and was followed up by two more, again at 78 r.p.m. One was Humphrey's *Hymn to God the Father* and some Handel arias. The other was of two Dowland songs, *Flow my tears* and *In darkness let me dwell*. This time he was accompanied, unusually, on the guitar. It was played by another new acquaintance of his, Desmond Dupré.

Dupré had been playing the classical guitar from the age of twelve, having taken it up with the idea of somehow accompanying his mother, a violinist. He had been dissuaded from professional music and sent to read chemistry at Oxford. After graduating he had practised as a chemist for some time before throwing it up for music. He had considered himself a pianist for a while, then switched to the 'cello, which he studied at the Royal College of Music. At the college he had become enthusiastic for old instrumental music and had returned to his guitar in order to play lute music. He played one evening at a musical party, at which another guest was a fellow alto of Deller's at St Paul's, Duncan Thomson, now headmaster of Ripon Cathedral Choir School. Thomson reported enthusiastically to Deller. Dupré was then living at his brother's vicarage in Battersea, and arrangements were quickly made for Deller to go there and try some Dowland songs with him. The result so satisfied them that they made the first of what would be countless appearances together, and, soon after, the first of their many recordings.

The discovery of an artist with such understanding and facility for lutenist music as Dupré added a further dimension to Alfred Deller's art. His position as the supreme living interpreter of Purcell was assured. He was recognizably the finest cathedral alto in living memory. Now he could show what he could do amongst the neglected treasures of lute song.

English lute song—secular song to the accompaniment of the lute, played either by the singer himself or by another—owed its origins to Europe. Lacking a natural troubadour tradition of her own, England subsisted thinly in the way of secular music until the late sixteenth century on songs brought from abroad, or on home-composed music to French and Italian verses dealing chiefly with such emotional themes as love fulfilled or unrequited. These sentiments were ideally in tune with the great Elizabethan literary and musical renaissance; and what Spenser, Sidney and Shakespeare achieved with the sonnet, John Dowland and Thomas Campion did equally gloriously with the lute song. Dowland, in particular, was a virtuoso on the instrument, unrivalled in Europe. Some idea of the esteem in which he was held as performer and composer can be had from the sonnet, sometimes attributed to Shakespeare, written by Richard Barnfield 'To his friend Maister R. L., in praise of Musique and Poetrie', in 1598, the year following Dowland's publication of his 'First Booke of Songes, so made that all the parts together, or either of them severally, may be sung to the lute'.

> If Musique and sweet Poetrie agree,
> As they must needes (the Sister and the Brother),
> Then must the Love be great, twixt thee and mee,
> Because thou lov'st the one, and I the other.
> *Dowland* to thee is deare; whose heavenly tuch
> Upon the Lute, doth ravish humaine sense:
> *Spenser* to mee; whose deepe Conceit is such,
> As, passing all Conceit, needs no defence.
> Thou lov'st to heare the sweete melodious sound,
> That *Phoebus* Lute (the Queen of Musique) makes:
> And I in deepe Delight am chiefly drownd
> When as himselfe to singing he betakes.
>> One God is God of Both (as Poets faigne),
>> One Knight loves Both, and Both in thee remaine.

Dowland is said to have been a countertenor himself. Whether this is true or not, the voice certainly filled an important place in the music of the time, and the combination of lyricism and sadness in his great songs *Flow my tears, Sorrow stay* and *In darkness let me dwell* is ideally expressed by it. The revival of this type of song, most highly representative of that time when English composers were unsurpassed anywhere, yet without taint of the archaic about it when listened to today, is very much due to Deller's advent.

Not that, having met Dupré, he now discovered the lutenists. For years he had been working for his own satisfaction with the songs of Dowland, Campion, and others, practising them, thinking about them, but never really believing that he would have the chance to sing them in public. As a result, when he and Desmond Dupré began to perform the lutenists they did so with an already perfected art whose impact could only be irresistible. As Deller says, 'My big opportunities have come to me relatively late in life, because of my late start as a professional, and Peggy has sometimes said, understandably, "If only it could all have happened ten years earlier." But none of it *could* have happened before it did. If it had, I would not have been ready and I wouldn't have known exactly what I wanted to do with, for instance, the songs of Purcell or Dowland. As I look back over my life I trace with astonishment the logical pattern of progress it has followed, with every significant coming together of persons or events occurring at precisely the right moment. I sensed when I was a boy that this would be so, and although I've had my moments of doubt, and thought that things were not going to work out any further, they always have.

'As I say, I quite literally didn't have to stop and think what I wanted to do with these songs when my chance to sing them came: I already knew. Now, I had come to singing absolutely as a natural thing, as an instinctive thing, and ever since I had been left very much to my own devices. As a result, my interpretations are entirely the product of my own instinct and thought, and I've been rebuked by certain critics and musicologists over the years for taking liberties with rhythms and notes and being too individual in my phrasing—these are the "Dellerisms" they talk about. But I must say that, having read more deeply in recent years about the music of those earlier centuries, I am satisfied that what instinct told me to do was right, and made me approach the songs in precisely the way their composers approached them.

'I can quote three interesting authorities who bear this out. Frescobaldi, writing in the preface to his Toccatas, almost half a century before Purcell's birth, speaks of, "Time taken now slowly, now swiftly, and even held in the air, according to the expression of the music, or the sense of the words." Then there's that interesting writer Thomas Mace, who published *Music's Monument* in 1676 and said, "When we come to be masters, so that we can command all manner of time at our own pleasure; we then take liberty . . . to break time; sometimes faster, and sometimes slower, as we perceive the nature of the thing required." And finally there's John Playford the elder, in his *Introduction to the Skill of Musick*, 1654: "I call that the noble manner of singing, which is used without tying a man's self to the ordinary manner of time, making many times the value of the notes less by half, and sometimes more, according to the conceit of the words."

'I agree that one can spoil a song by bending its rhythm *too much*. I think that rhythm is of the first importance in singing, whether the song is a miniature piece lasting a minute or an aria lasting eight minutes. Every song has a basic, underlying rhythm which I call its ground swell, and one must be conscious of this from the first note to the last. One has to carry this ground swell in the mind and relate every variation of rhythm and tempo to it. And the key to defining the ground swell is, in my opinion, the text of the song: the poetry of the words.

'Both in Dowland and in Purcell the setting of the English language is perfect. In a Purcell song of the perfection of *Music for a while* it is impossible, I think, to sense which was composed first, the music or the words. They are wedded so perfectly, so subtly, that one can't believe that any other note could be possible for that particular word or syllable. This is also true of Dowland. One could look through the entire literature of Dowland and not find any instance of false emphasis, a strong beat on a weak syllable. Of course, we know that Dowland wrote some of his greatest songs entirely himself, music and words, and performed them—as a countertenor, some authorities believe—to his own lute accompaniment. Not all the lutenist composers could do that, but their composition reflects an age in which music and words were required to serve and enhance one another. The countertenor was the most important voice in this Golden Age, and the three together made what was regarded as the perfect trinity.

'I have been told by people that because this fusion in

such songs *is* perfect, the singer's only function is to sing them at a given or accepted tempo, sticking strictly to what the composer set down, and the result must be a perfect interpretation. My feeling, and absolute conviction, is that you cannot possibly take such a song as Purcell's *Sweeter than roses*, or any other great rhapsodic song, just sing the notes, at whatever tempo, and do justice to it. The whole mood of the words is what must predominate, and my approach is entirely through my feeling, my emotional feeling, for those words.

'One must make the words live in a way personal to oneself, and the rhythms get changed instinctively.

'The same applies to ornamentation. The whole purpose of ornamentation is to heighten the emotive quality of the text. But if you have to work away at a cadenza, with everything coming to a stop while you take a great breath and launch off on a clever display, it becomes unnatural and defeats its end. If you are singing *'Tis nature's voice*—'Tis nature's voice, through all the *moving* woods . . . —and you have ornamentation, or coloratura, on the word "moving", then you must move the voice quickly through it in such a way that you get the feeling of vitality. That is the whole purpose.

'It is recorded that Purcell, when composing one of his odes, could hear a chorister being rehearsed in one of his songs in another room. The singing master kept stopping the boy and trying to make him sing the ornaments exactly as Purcell had put them down on paper. Purcell called out, "Leave the boy alone. He will ornament by nature better than you or I can tell him." This is my whole approach to rhythm. If what I am singing sounds to the listener as being something which is produced, as it were, out of the air, for him, for this moment, then I have succeeded completely in what I meant to do.'

Inevitably, this emotive, instinctive approach, which, coupled with the unique quality of his voice, makes Deller so distinctive and distinguished an artist, is what has most offended his more pedantic hearers. Another 'Dellerism' with which he is charged is his practice of making a slight crescendo on the voice to an upper note, then thinning out the sound to piano or pianissimo. At best, it can be hauntingly successful; at worst, an obtrusive mannerism.

Deller says, 'I know perfectly well that I have this mannerism, which some people feel is affected. I can only say that it isn't. Once again, it is a product of instinct arising from the mood of what I am singing as inspired by the words. I do it to heighten the poetic meaning of a particular phrase, not to produce what I think is a pretty sound. The fact that my voice is higher than most other males' is of no importance to me. Again, I know that some people object to some occasional facial expressions when I sing, and to my tendency to gesticulate slightly with my hands and sometimes beat the time. One friend says he would prefer it if I sang from behind a screen. I can only repeat that everything I do comes quite naturally, and springs more from the music than from me. My mind is not on such external things as facial expression and gestures, and I don't see why I should take any steps to control these minor foibles (though I would check them in a student). Standing absolutely still all the time is for me unnatural.

'What matters is the ability to reach my listeners through the medium of the voice I have been given and the songs I sing with it: trying to convey to you something that is felt within me. I am not Alfred Deller, singer, standing up to perform a song; but Alfred Deller being used, if you like, to communicate with the listener on a very different plane from anything to do with technique.'

If the last remark comes perilously close to sounding like the grossest affectation of them all, anyone who has been close to Deller professionally or privately can supply reassurance. To go to the other extreme, it would be fanciful to portray him as a man possessed; an ancient soul reincarnated from the age whose music he so perfectly understands and projects, entranced beyond awareness of what he is about. Yet, that strong mystical

instinct which has underlain his life perhaps owes its
existence to something more than his religious experiences.
A less sincere, more self-conscious man might, indeed,
find it convenient to persuade himself and other people
that he is living proof of reincarnation. Deller claims
nothing of the sort, invents no memories, subjective or
atavistic, strikes no attitudes, does not deliberately
surround himself with the trappings of the times with
which he is so identified: the romantically beautiful old
house in which he lives is, one feels, a happy accident,
rather than a chosen setting; the beard which so enhances
his 'period' appearance owes its origin to a specific
occasion* and was retained because it was more right for
his face than the moustache which preceded it (and, sub-
consciously no doubt, as a permanent deterrent to
questions of masculinity). Yet, knowing him, it is sometimes hard to shake away a suspicion that only his body

---

* See p. 141.

belongs to the family into which he was born; that for all his bonhomie, warm good-will towards mankind and down-to-earth Christianity, his soul is something remote and untouchable, a spirit caught in flesh as Ariel was imprisoned in the tree—only to more purpose. His humour, great as it is, seems to be the bright edge round a cloud of that pervading, dominant melancholy which haunts Elizabethan and Jacobean poetry, music and thought. Out of company, he is ready prey to depression and brooding melancholy, as he readily admits:

'When I wake in the morning is my most vulnerable time. The longer I lie in bed, the worse my depression becomes, and it always works round to the same things: personal failure in relationships, unworthiness, the dread thought of having to retire or give up working for any other reason, the terrible idea of dying, the awful prospect of infinity. This may seem at odds with my religious convictions, but it's something I can't help and which, at times, seems capable of overwhelming me completely.'

His depressions—rarer, fortunately, or less apparent, than his bursts of gaiety—are familiar to all who have been closest to him. His dark vein of melancholy, as much as his poetic sensibility, brings him into immediate sympathy with the Elizabethans. There is something in it of their morbidity: the skull, poisoned and masked like a lady, in *The Revenger's Tragedy*; Mary Stuart's dainty watch in the form of a *memento mori*; Cecil's tomb at Hatfield, with its sculpted decomposing corpse; the block and axe on Tower Hill, ever in the minds of Tudor nobles, and the gibbet and pestilence looming over the common folk. It haunted their poetry and their music: *In darkness let me dwell*; *Flow not so fast, sad fountains*; *Woeful heart with grief oppressed*; *Flow, flow, my tears. . . .* Dowland and the lutenists gave them their highest expression, and they form the most personally identified portion of Alfred Deller's repertoire.

He says: 'Reincarnation? Mystical basis? I prefer the expression "cheating time". Just occasionally—and the occasions are rare enough to remember—one achieves so perfect an involvement with the music, the words, the mood, the message, if you like, of what is being sung, and with one's hearers themselves, that there comes a feeling of complete identification and the end of personality and the meaning of time. One is outside time, out in eternity, where a gap of mere centuries is so meaningless that it ceases to exist, and so is bridged. This is the most intense, most marvellous experience I or any other artist can undergo.'

In retrieving the long-lost glories of Purcell, in communicating the Elizabethan art song in a way in which it has not been heard since the days of its origin, if then, and in touching with fresh magic the works of Bach, Handel and other composers of the Baroque period, Alfred Deller has not failed to keep in touch with earthier musical forms. His repertoire includes many examples of British folk song, and, once more, his rare voice type is able to reveal qualities which have gone unappreciated in more standard performances. Though his sound is unmistakably masculine, and his approach to all that he sings is manly, that ability to convey intense emotion without sense of sexual stress which makes his voice so priceless a gift to Tudor song is a boon also to folk song. There is in his renderings of such songs as *Blow away the morning dew*, *Strawberry Fair* or *Greensleeves* none of that coy, olde Englishe quaintness of so many renderings. The frank, inoffensive bawdry which still lingers in the words of many folk songs, despite the bowdlerizations of collectors, sounds self-conscious on the lips of most men and quite out of place on a woman's. Deller could sing, if he chose—and sometimes he does choose—the most outrageous of early tavern songs without offence, his sense of period making them sound as natural and unremarkable to modern ears as they were to contemporary ones. The tragedy and starkness of 'Merrie England' are conveyed vividly to us in his interpretation of such a ballad as *Lord Randall*, *The Lover's Ghost* or *King Henry* without recourse to violence of tone or exaggerated expression. That other-worldly quality of his voice puts such things into a perspective we have not before seen. It is not a case of playing Beethoven on the harmonica, or Bartók on the tubular bells. Historically, Alfred Deller is re-creating, not originating. He brings back something once familiar, novel only because of long absence. He says, 'Many of the folk songs are as old as, or older than, the art songs, the lute songs, of the Elizabethans, and the more lyrical examples, such as *Waly Waly*, I've always felt one must treat in exactly the same way as one would treat the art songs. They're often beautiful melodies with very touching words, the product of natural art. The countertenor voice is no more necessarily connected with folk song than is any other one type of voice, but again there is the historical fact that the countertenor was widely used when those songs were being most sung, and that it is particularly suited to expressing those elements of pathos and poignancy which one finds in so many of them.'

Naturally, the sense of period which had drawn him so straight and surely to the lute songs before he could see any chance of performing them attracted him also to the even richer field of the madrigal. Here, he found a distinct function for the countertenor.

'As a preface to his *Psalmes, Sonets, & Songs of Sadnes and Pietie*, in 1588, William Byrd wrote, "If thou delight in music of great compass here are divers songs which being originally made for instruments to express the harmony and one voice to pronounce the ditty are now framed in all parts for voices to sing the same." This reference to great compass is interesting, for a large part of all madrigal literature involves the employment of two countertenor voices, often required to span close upon two octaves. This has posed a problem for the modern editor, and is usually solved by the redistribution of the parts—that is, when a part would seem to be too high for the tenor it is given to the alto, and when too low for the alto, to the tenor. This is a practical solution, since the important thing is to have these masterpieces performed, even if countertenors are not available. Still, it is preferable to have at least one countertenor.'

It was Deller's concern to give the madrigal its ideal expression that led him into a course of action for which the world may thank him.

Soon after he had begun broadcasting for the B.B.C., sometimes performing ensemble works with other singers who were also soloists in their own right, he realized that what was needed ideally was a group of singers accustomed to working together *as* an ensemble: people with a sense of an especial style, and with the desired mental approach, who could subjugate individuality to the work in hand.

'This arose from one or two miserable experiences,' he recalls. 'There were four or five of us, singing our heads off, with no question of an agreed balance, so that what we did made no sense at all. I came to feel that, given the opportunity and the occasion, I would like to collect my own singers who could work together regularly, get to know one another intimately and become a really cohesive team. I knew that the madrigal was essentially an intimate thing, to be performed ideally in the familiar surroundings of a great house by members of a family, or friends, singing together from the part books: people who knew each other in an intimate way, and could predict one another and compromise with one another to achieve perfect harmony. Also, I saw the madrigal as a kind of little masterpiece of vocal chamber music which could be approached in the same way and with the same musical discipline as a string quartet works. I felt that it would be possible with five or six individual voices, rehearsing five or six individual strands of music in the way that a chamber music ensemble rehearses, to achieve more real intensity than could be got from a small choir, however well chosen.'

His first venture in this direction was the formation of the Amphion Ensemble, consisting of Deller, April Cantelo, soprano, Harry Barnes, tenor, Norman Platt, baritone, Walter Bergmann, harpsichord and piano, Desmond Dupré, viola da gamba and guitar, and, usually, a violinist and perhaps a flautist. It was not a long-lived association. All of them had engagements of their own to keep, while opportunities of appearing together were rare.

What they did do, though, they did successfully; and what he had learned from the experiment emboldened Deller to form his now famous Consort.

This was in 1950. To begin with it was to be an all-male group. Instinctively, he first looked amongst his colleagues in the choir stalls of St Paul's for men he already knew and liked, and whom he knew had experience of ensemble singing. He chose Maurice Bevan, a baritone with a deep interest in the music of the seventeenth century, who had joined the choir the year after him. Bevan is still a member of St Paul's choir today, and still a regular member of the Deller Consort.

The tenors he selected were Harry Barnes, from Westminster Abbey choir, and Eric Barnes (no relation), a colleague at St Paul's. The group had no name when it gave its first performance, a broadcast of Thomas Tallis's *Lamentation*. Before long it acquired two sopranos, April Cantelo and Eileen McLoughlin, and a name, the Deller Consort. 'I remember,' says Deller, 'we gave a concert in Stratford-on-Avon for Wilfrid Mellers, and he suggested some very high-flown name like "Cantorys Britannici". This didn't seem at all convincing, and I think it was in a conversation with Walter Bergmann that the idea came up of using my own name, on the theory that, as I was associated in the public's mind with music of a particular period, anyone reading that there was going to be a performance by the Deller Consort would know just what kind of thing to expect.'

The Deller Consort proved an immediate success. A number of broadcasting engagements brought it quickly to the notice of concert agents and it was soon well established on the music club circuit and on the lists of the organizers of Britain's proliferating music festivals. Its complement has seen a number of comings-and-goings, but its standards have remained constant, its reputation and Deller's moving side by side upon the heights. Whether it performs madrigals of the English and Italian schools, sacred music of thirteenth-century France, roistering tavern songs and glees from Elizabethan England, folk music, or, more rarely, works from the nineteenth and twentieth centuries, some of them specially composed for it, its qualities are unvarying. It has performed in many countries, and been acclaimed in them all as the most perfect musical combination of its kind that it is possible to conceive. Its many recordings

have earned every kind of praise whenever they have appeared, and the award of the Grand Prix du Disque in 1965 for the French Harmonia Mundi issue of Orazio Vecchi's Commedia Dell'Arte, *L'Amfiparnaso* (1597).*

There is, however, no such thing as *the* Deller Consort. A hopeless dream of Deller's is to be able to retain the same constant group, again in the manner of the instrumental ensembles; always rehearsing, travelling and performing together in unbroken intimacy, perhaps with

---

* The German Harmonia Mundi issue, in 1961, had been awarded the German critics' prize.

their own permanent combination of musicians, who would use the contemporary instruments which add immeasurably to the performance of baroque and earlier music. It is an impossible ideal, both financially and because, like Deller himself, the other members like to leaven their ensemble work with the solo engagements for which they are in constant demand. Thus, the Consort's make-up varies from tour to tour, sometimes from concert to concert; but in getting on for twenty years of existence it has continued to draw upon a limited number of artists possessing that rather rare type of temperament which can merge itself self-effacingly into vocal chamber music. In addition to those already mentioned, these have included sopranos Eileen Poulter, Honor Sheppard, Mary Thomas, Sally le Sage and Suzanne Green, tenors Wilfred Brown, Gerald English, Alexander Young, Robert Tear, Max Worthley, Philip Todd, John Buttrey and Neil Jenkins, baritone Norman Platt, and, as additional countertenor, Deller's own son, Mark.

If the Deller Consort always achieves top results, it does so not only because of Deller, but also in spite of him. Instinctive genius leads him unhesitatingly to the very core of a song's musical and poetic unity. His is the approach of the poet who has been given music, rather than literature, through which to express his sentiments, and in ensemble, as well as in solo work, he does not hesitate to take liberties with rhythm and tempo. It can be disconcerting to a fellow performer not privy to his tricks.

'Anybody who joins the Consort as a new member is sitting on a razor's edge for about his first year, if not longer,' a colleague declares. 'There were times when I thought, "I'll have to give it up", because everyone else was used to anticipating Alfred's next move, and I wasn't. When you come in you have to learn a sizeable amount of music pretty suddenly, and the trouble is you don't get the rehearsal because he doesn't like rehearsing. He leaves it to the feeling of the performance. He will let all kinds of things go at rehearsal, and rely on you when the time comes to know what it's all about and respond to what he wants. It can be terrifying, but perhaps it is all to the good, in the long run. It heightens the emotional intensity, gives an air of desperation, or something, to the performance, when we suddenly feel the tongues of fire descending from Heaven like the Pentecostal experience. This is a familiar thing to us, and I think a great deal of it is due to his magnetism. We love the music as much as he does, and we all like Alfred very much indeed, so that we respond to one another when the time comes, whatever misgivings we've had before.

'I remember a concert we had to give in Bruges which we dreaded, because we had had a heavy and tiring time of recording sessions in the South of France, and an impossibly tight schedule. We had to travel by car from where we were staying into Nice at five in the morning, fly to Brussels, take a train for Bruges, and be on the platform within about an hour of arrival. We all felt half dead, and were grumbling amongst ourselves about Alfred ever having accepted the job and there having been no chance to rehearse. We went on to the platform of an ancient hall, hardly knowing what we were doing, and straight away we found ourselves singing in a most marvellous acoustic. That performance of Byrd's five-part Mass was unforgettable because we struck that acoustic, Alfred responded to it immediately, and we responded to him. Although we rely on each other so completely, we rely upon Alfred most. If he gives, we respond, even in the most unlikely programmes which seem at first to be too long and chronologically haphazard. In a mysterious way, they come off, partly, I think, due to this magnetism of Alfred's. He's very much the slave of his feelings. If he is feeling below par, he can't understand how anyone else can possibly be feeling well. The result is that we all finish up feeling below par. If we all feel terrible, but he feels good, then we draw strength from him and recover straight away.'

Another member of the Consort says, 'One of the most

disconcerting things for a newcomer is that this instinct of his for rhythmic shape can result in quite a different performance from what has been rehearsed. When he sings a solo it always goes much slower than one might expect. When one of us sings a solo, and he is conducting, he almost always goes faster than one wants to go. He feels the excitement of the music, but doesn't have to manage it technically, and so he pushes us on. I sometimes feel, "For heaven's sake, stop pushing me. This is the speed I want, and I'm not going to look at you."'

To which Deller replies, 'I know that some of my colleagues feel this very strongly, as I would under other conductors. To that extent, I admit it. But, in my own defence, I must add that in conducting I am always conscious first of all of what a singer wants in the way of time for breathing, and so on, and my demands are realistic. What I am relentless about, though, is in insisting that this strong conviction I have about the way the piece should go must be obeyed. If I seem to drive, it is in order to wring out the music in the way I want it to come. Of course, the Consort understand and expect this, though we have differed on occasions. When I conduct other ensembles or orchestras, where you might expect there to be some difficulty, I must say I've always been given the performance I wanted. If there were objections at rehearsal, I should still insist, but give my reasons for doing so. I wouldn't stalk out in a rage.'

And the Consort members respond, 'You learn from experience that there are times to stand up to him, and times to hold your counsel. He'll get his own way if you don't argue. When you do he may resent it at the time, but he'll often come round to your point of view later.'

Desmond Dupré, who has accompanied Deller more than anyone, accepts his lot philosophically. 'Alfred likes to sing a song or two before the concert, just to get his vocal chords moving, but he certainly doesn't care for much in the way of rehearsal. Even when he does condescend to go through a song beforehand, it doesn't mean all that much in terms of the actual performance. If we were to rehearse Morley's *It was a lover and his lass* only five minutes before going on stage, and then were to do it as our first item, it would still come out differently from what we'd just done. Invariably, he sings it about five per cent faster in performance, and I always try to stop him, because the rehearsal speed is about as fast as it's possible to play it on the lute. All the same, I find it less difficult to accompany him than to play with people who are basically rhythmic, yet take unmusical pauses to breathe, and so on. No one I've been with has taken more liberties with rhythm than Alfred; yet I can see the purpose of, and the rightness of everything he does, and therefore I don't find him hard to accompany.'

It is not only in musical matters that Deller's associates have had to come to terms with him. Though not given to the temperamental outbursts traditionally associated with singers, he can be moody and, at times, obtuse, especially on tour. One of his recurrent worries is that his stamina may not see him through to the end. He feels that he begins a tour with a certain stock of resources which he must husband carefully if they are to last out. Any unexpected demands he has to face are seen as an extra drain upon this supply, and provoke melancholy ruminations. He watches himself and his health so intently that the result is near-hypochondria and a tendency to see alarming portents in small discomforts. He is convinced that a Deller must inevitably suffer either from a chronic back or a weak stomach, and, unable to claim the former, has settled for the latter. Actually, his constitution is superb, but that his gastric juices govern much of his life is not imagination. He is neither gourmand nor gourmet, but nothing puts him into a worse frame of mind than a bad meal, or, even worse, no meal at all at the appointed time. If there is to be argument over a point of performance, anyone but a complete stranger knows the futility of embarking on it just before a mealtime. Afterwards, when the juices are flowing satisfactorily, is

the moment. He eats small amounts, and prefers plain food; but it must be served promptly, or, in his view, it will do him no good at all.

Maurice Bevan, who, in the absence of any professional manager, attends to the Consort's travelling arrangements, recalls the time in Germany when they found themselves at Dortmund between trains. Knowing his man of old, Bevan had carefully booked a connection which would allow them the best part of two hours for a leisurely meal. Unhappily, there proved to be no restaurant in immediate view. His expression aghast, Deller simply put down his bags and said, 'Well, where is it?', leaving his colleagues to bustle off in every direction looking for food. At length, Max Worthley returned with the news that just round the corner was a buffet where fresh milk could be obtained. 'Milk?' came the agonized cry. 'Milk isn't a meal!' Eventually the station restaurant, badly sited, was found. The day and Maurice Bevan's reputation were saved.

Deller eats little, if anything, before a concert, with the result that by the time it ends he wants nothing more urgently than a strong drink and some food. This being a need common to most artists, both are usually forthcoming, though an occasional thoughtless or disorganized host has allowed introductions and prolonged conversation to intrude. Then Deller, who can be the most charming and grateful of guests, grows more and more perfunctory in his responses. He has been heard to growl, 'If there's no food on the table in ten minutes, I'm off.' He has sometimes kept his word.

Today, with many tours at home and abroad behind him, he sums up his experience of hospitality generally as: on the Continent, considerate and well managed, often in the welcome form of an arranged visit to a good restaurant immediately after the performance, with no reception to attend; in America, most generous and well-meant, but overwhelming and often more taxing than enjoyable; in Britain, too often non-existent, with concert organizers considering their obligations over when the performance ends—a state of affairs sadly familiar to many other singers, actors, speakers, and 'performers' in public, though most have experienced delightful exceptions. One of Deller's most memorable occurred in England some years ago when the Consort was engaged to give a recital in an arts festival at Chester, for a fee which was to include accommodation for the night. Deller, whose ways with correspondence are vague and forgetful, registered nothing in his mind about the arrangements, save that he and Desmond Dupré were to be the charge of a certain host, while their colleagues went elsewhere. When afternoon rehearsal finished he was not surprised to be told that the car for himself and Dupré was waiting outside, and was only mildly staggered to find that it was an olive green Rolls-Royce, the largest he had seen in his life. After a drive of half-an-hour or so the uniformed chauffeur turned the car off the road into a private drive which wound for what appeared to be the best part of a mile to the front door of a magnificent house. An elegant lady—'straight out of *Vogue*' is Deller's description—emerged to greet them, followed by a butler who carried off their baggage. As they entered the hall, they noticed the magnificence of the paintings which lined the main stairway, and it occurred to each of them that it would be nice to own such fine copies of Gainsborough, Velasquez, and an assortment of other masters.

After tea in a superb drawing-room, their still-anonymous hostess, who had officiated with supreme charm, told them, 'Now, I'm not giving you a heavy meal now. We'll have dinner here quietly after the concert. Meanwhile, I'm going to be really firm with you and tell George to take you to your rooms and run your baths, so that you will have plenty of time to rest and get ready. I've put Mr Dupré into the Blue Room, and you, Mr Deller, into the Primrose.'

Deller recalls, 'By now, both Desmond and I were beginning to wonder quite where we were. As we got up to follow George, a door opened and an imposing gentleman entered with eight dogs. We had some conversation with him, and, again, there was absolute charm, but no clue to identity. So Desmond was taken off to his room and I to mine, which turned out to have a four-poster bed with primrose hangings to match the primrose carpet and curtains. Imagine my feelings as I went through my door and found that George had been thorough to a fault. He'd unpacked my bag and laid out my partially worn dress shirt, my suit and my dirty socks. The private bathroom was all primrose yellow, too.* The entire contents of my toilet-bag had been emptied on to a shelf, squeezed-out tube of toothpaste and all. I just stood and looked, and I heard a strangulated voice behind me. It was Desmond, standing in the doorway, saying, "Alfred! Isn't it shaming?"'

They discovered later that they had been staying with the Duke and Duchess of Westminster; and that the Gainsboroughs, Velasquez, and the rest, were *not* copies.

One of Deller's first experiences of American hospitality, again in the most select of surroundings, had a more dramatic outcome. It was at that most superior of ladies' colleges, Sweet Briar, Virginia. At a post-performance party Deller had his first experience of drinking Bourbon, of which he accepted several well-filled tumblers, whose contents he innocently assumed to include a good proportion of water. He was not the first to have fallen into this trap for beginners, nor the last to pass out on standing up too abruptly. The massive form fell straight into the arms of Dupré and the diminutive harpsichordist Robert Conant. With assistance, they bore it to the best bedroom in the Director of Music's house, where it lay, motionless, until morning. Having breakfasted—'the one and only time I've had breakfast in tails'—Deller's problem was to get back to his room in the

---

* Dupré recalls in his an eighteenth-century elbow-chair arranged over the lavatory pan, and on a table a packet of toilet paper, in a delicate saucer held in position by a decorated glass paperweight.

Almost everywhere it performs in the world, but most especially in America, France and Germany, the Deller Consort can be certain of more than average enthusiasm for its coming, and of rapt attention from its audiences. The exception, again, is in Britain, ironically the cradle of the great music which Deller has helped to restore to life. Michael Tippett explains, 'One has to remember that it is not only Alfred who has experienced this contrast between the reception he gets abroad and at home. Nobody who hasn't been to Germany to perform English polyphonic music, for instance, has any idea what an excitement it is to the Germans. They are musical people, it is wonderful music, and they've never heard it before. When Alfred goes there with the Consort it's an absolute knock-out. In this country there isn't the novelty. The heyday of the discovery of our own music is a little earlier, and so we've had more experience of it. In America it's different again. You have that vast country, with vast distances between the centres in which you perform. The university campuses are very wealthy, with an expert on baroque music on nearly every one of them and a study of baroque that is almost continuous, so that there's a tremendously receptive field. Here, there's nothing of that kind at all.'

It was an American girl student who paid Deller the compliment he treasures above all others: his singing, she declared, left her feeling 'all clean inside'. But the most unexpectedly appreciative reception he and the Consort have ever experienced occurred in Australia and New Zealand, during their 1964 visit, the first vocal ensemble to do so. Deller admits, 'I went with all the built-in prejudices about these countries being back of beyond, cultureless, and so on; and on each and every point I was shown up to the hilt how wrong I was. We went under the auspices of Musica Viva, which is the only society throughout Australia arranging chamber concerts. In every city we played we broke Musica Viva's box-office records; and the most incredible thing to me was that two-thirds of our audiences were young people. The sort of youth you would expect to be yelling their heads off for beat groups were queueing to come into our concerts.

'In Sydney Town Hall we performed our normal sort of programme—Byrd's five-part Mass, Italian and English madrigals, French chansons—to an audience of eighteen hundred. So many were turned away that Musica Viva had to arrange a return concert for us to give when we got back from our New Zealand tour. I remember, we arrived back at Sydney's airport from New Zealand one Sunday night, dead tired, and we had just gone through with our baggage when a porter said to me, "There's a bit of a surprise for you out there." We went through the door, and there was the place packed with young people, holding an enormous banner, "Welcome Back to the Deller Consort". It was most incredible and marvellous.'

It was markedly different from the reception they had had when arriving to take part in a performance of the Monteverdi Vespers in Paris. It was to take place in the church of Les Invalides, and a Radio-Télévision Française car was to pick them up at their hotel at 9 a.m. and drive them to a studio for a 10 a.m. rehearsal. Only one member of the party was missing, Mary Thomas, the soprano, who was flying from England and had arranged to meet them at the studio.

At the appointed hour a shooting brake arrived and they piled in and were driven off. After some time they began to pass through what were obviously the outskirts of Paris, and then reached a motorway, down which they proceeded to travel at high speed. Confidently, Deller reassured his colleagues that they would arrive at the studio at any moment, and almost at once the car began to slow down. It halted at the entrance to a forbidding-looking place surrounded by barbed wire, with armed sentries marching up and down. In his non-existent French, Deller sought reassurance from the driver.

'Radio?'

'Zackly.'

This they interpreted to mean 'exactly', so that when they were driven inside and then ushered out of the car into a sort of guard room they were able confidently to accept Max Worthley's theory that no doubt the radio station had to be extra carefully guarded after all those Algerian troubles. The precautions seemed to be thorough indeed, to the extent of a Security-like scrutiny of their papers, during which Worthley wandered across to the girl receptionist to ask if their other soprano had arrived yet. Her face assumed an expression he could not quite interpret. The other officials, already apparently mystified about something, began to register obvious alarm, turning to dismay when Worthley mentioned a performance of the Monteverdi Vespers. The girl seized the telephone and embarked upon a series of increasingly agitated calls, leaving someone else to explain what appeared to have happened. . . .

How that morning was spent by the party of British scientists who had been due to be picked up by a car at that same hotel, and at that same time, to be driven to the Atomic Research Station at Saclay, has never been revealed.

TEN

In 1959, while he was still at St Paul's, Deller received a letter from Suffolk:

THE RED HOUSE, ALDEBURGH, SUFFOLK

18th August, 1959

My dear Alfred,

As you may know, we are planning to rebuild our Jubilee Hall here, and with any luck it should be ready for its reopening in the Festival next year. I am planning to write a new opera for this rather grand occasion, and it looks as if the subject will be the Midsummer Night's Dream (I am keeping this quiet at the moment because journalists are curious animals, and seize on this kind of story in a way which is occasionally embarrassing). I wonder how you would react to the idea of playing Oberon in this? It is for a big cast, and each group of people has to be carefully calculated vocally. I see you and hear your voice very clearly in this part, but before I start to write it I should love to know your reactions, and perhaps you can let us know how you are placed in May and June next year. We hope to give four or five performances in the Festival, between June 11th and 26th, and we should rehearse for four or five weeks beforehand. We would also probably do some performances abroad and in London later.

Do let me know what you feel!

Yours ever

Ben

Dear Ben,

It has taken me two days to recover from the shock! After all, my only stage experience was with the Church Dramatic Society, six performances of 'Laburnam [*sic*] Grove', and I was young then, and my mind (pardon the word) much more alert. Do you and Peter think I could do it? If so, I would consider it a privilege to make the attempt.

Yours,

Alfred

THE RED HOUSE, ALDEBURGH, SUFFOLK

Monday

Dear Alfred,

We do *indeed* think you can do it, and more, that you will be triumphantly successful in it! You can trust Ben, I think, to write you a lovely vocal part. Your height and presence will be absolutely right (—so will your beard!) and the part will probably be a rather static one—I mean

139

you won't be required to turn cartwheels or climb trees—and it would be wonderful to have you with us.

Ben mentioned dates didn't he? 1st night June 11th with a month's rehearsals before, the last two weeks of them in Aldeburgh probably. The Festival itself is June 11-25. There would be five performances in the Festival (with other things for you I expect) and perhaps performances in London and abroad later on.

Ben is delighted that you will do it. So am I, dear Alfred, and most grateful.

Yours ever

Peter

His correspondents were, of course, Benjamin Britten and Peter Pears, with both of whom he had been associated in concert work at various times. It was perhaps the best piece of unexpected news Deller had received in his life. He had no reason to suppose that it would lead to his life's greatest disappointment.

The following summer he received his vocal part for *A Midsummer Night's Dream* and was delighted. He felt that Britten had perfectly linked his voice with the character of Oberon, whom he had invested with a Prospero-like dignity. In particular, the quiet setting of *I know a bank* struck him as a masterpiece of modern lyricism. The musical rehearsals proceeded, so far as he was concerned, smoothly and happily.

The rehearsals on the tiny stage of the Jubilee Hall itself left him a shade less confident. John Cranko's production seemed to Deller perfunctory, so far as his own part was concerned, though he had been warned that his role would not require him to act much, and he could appreciate that Cranko had bigger things to worry about in managing capering rustics, boy fairies, a boy acrobat as Puck, and all the rest of a largish cast, in a setting of cramped woodland. Perhaps understandably, the question of 'what to do with Deller' seemed to bear fairly low priority.

For all his great gift of mimicry and his youthful interest in amateur dramatics, both as actor and producer, Alfred Deller had—and has—never wanted to dress up and act. It needs little perception to see that he would not make much success of it. His mimicry flares up suddenly and spontaneously out of a conversation, burns brilliantly for a little while, then is just as quickly gone. He would be incapable of the sustained, disciplined effort of acting. The suggestion which has been made from time to time that he and the Consort might assume costume to heighten the period atmosphere of some of their recitals he has always rejected as irrelevant and undesirable. One exception had been in 1955 when he and Desmond Dupré had undertaken to take part in a re-creation of an Elizabethan musical evening arranged by the wife of Sir Herbert Read in the contemporary setting of Hovingham Hall, Yorkshire, the home of Colonel Sir William Worsley. Having agreed, with some misgivings, to wear Elizabethan dress, Deller, accompanied by Peggy, went along to a London theatrical costumier's for a fitting. When he had donned his costume the fitter produced a small beard and popped it experimentally on to his then clean-shaven chin. On the way home Peggy remarked how well the beard had suited him, and during a caravan holiday in Ireland that summer he grew his own, which has remained with him ever since.

His only other costume appearance was in Australia in 1965 when *The Play of Daniel* was presented in Adelaide. 'He stood like a rogue elephant,' one of his colleagues remembers. 'He looked magnificent, until he moved, and then it was all wrong. He seemed to run amok. He lifted up the seven-branched candlestick of the Temple, which was supposed to be a very heavy piece of furniture, like a piece of cork, and thrust it at one as though he was going to push one off the stage with it.'

Opinions about Deller's stage presence in *A Midsummer Night's Dream* vary between extremes. Some critics found him uninspiring, some undramatic, some wooden. Some praised his singing; but too many for his comfort concentrated on his alleged shortcomings as an actor. More than one professional colleague has suggested

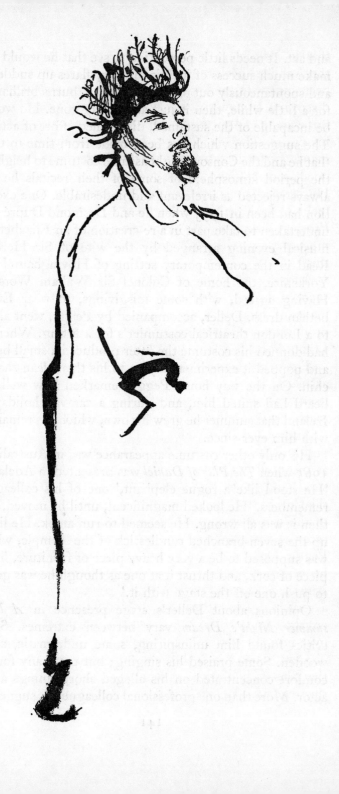

that in venturing upon a stage Deller at last revealed the Achilles' heel of which he and his critics had so far been unaware, and that they made the most of the discovery. It may have been true in one or two instances, but even the fairest-minded of critics found little to say in his praise. Michael Tippett, however, found his performance perfectly satisfying: 'I thought he was extremely good, and that it didn't matter at all that he couldn't act. He seemed to me to convey a tremendously dignified feeling. I thought that Britten had wanted to put a Prospero-like character over, and turn Oberon into a much stronger character, and Alfred had, in fact, achieved this.'

Anthony Lewis says, 'I think it was an eminently successful idea to cast him, and in the limited demands made of him he was quite sufficiently effective. The production seemed to me sensitive and sympathetic, and I thought he made a suitably commanding figure.'

The printed criticisms dismayed Deller for a time; but, as usual, his depression was not long-lived. The opera itself was widely praised, and Britten himself was well pleased with Deller's part in it.

After its brief Aldeburgh Festival run the company performed *A Midsummer Night's Dream* again successfully at the Holland Festival and began to plan their professional and private engagements round the dates fixed for the Covent Garden season at which it was to be presented to the world at large. Then, one day, Michael Tippett received what he terms an 'agonized' telephone call from Peggy. Deller had just had word through his agents that he was not, after all, wanted at Covent Garden. The American Russell Oberlin, whose voice was more that of a very high tenor than of a true countertenor, had been engaged in his place. The news had bowled Deller clean over into the blackest depression of his life, Peggy told Tippett, who recalls: 'He was quite sure that this meant that the Aldeburgh people had betrayed him, that all they had said to him was false. I spoke to him and told him that I didn't think this was so; but I explained that, false or not, this was a situation which very often occurs in our profession. You can go out as fast as you go in. I said, "Everybody's in this boat; you can't expect anything else." However, I promised to try to resolve the issue for him. I think, in fact, I asked Covent Garden about it, and it turned out to be the other way round: Britten had threatened not to have anything further to do with the production because Alfred had been turned out. It was Covent Garden who wanted Oberlin, and Britten did not. He was furious that this was so, and had given his permission very reluctantly, but, for some reason or other, hadn't written to Alfred to explain. I told Alfred all this, but his depression was extreme. He thought the whole world had been cut from under his feet."*

Deller says, 'It was certainly the low spot of my life. I think I sang in the first performance at Aldeburgh as well as I'm capable of singing; so it was depressing to receive such a panning from the critics. As to the acting, well, I went to those rehearsals with an absolutely open mind and put myself completely into the producer's hands. What he asked me to do I did to the best of my ability, though, looking back, I think that a lot of it was wrong. I'm quite sure that I would have made a better impression from the acting point of view if I'd been treated rather more majestically, with statuesque exits and entrances and less moving around on the stage. After all, I'm an enormous man for a tiny stage like the Jubilee Hall's, and trying to sweep round in that confined space, knowing how cramped you are, doesn't enable you to move with any confidence.'

Fortunately, his natural resilience, together with the reassurances of Peggy and professional colleagues, pre-

---

* *Authors' Note :* Owing to pressure of work Mr Benjamin Britten was not able to comment on the incident, other than to say that his admiration for Alfred Deller's performance has since been confirmed by his choice of him for the recording of the work made in London in November 1966 (*see* Discography).

vented any lapsing into self-pity and quickly restored his confidence in himself. He has never since appeared in any rôle requiring him to act: the Achilles' heel has remained firmly concealed. There is no doubt that he would like to have sung Oberon at Covent Garden, and he is certain that he would have done so with success. What the unhappy business has not done, fortunately, has been to leave him with any outsize chip on his shoulder with regard to critics in general, although he sees himself as especially vulnerable to them:

'Even critics have inbred prejudices, like the rest of us, and in some cases, I tend to think, more so. "We have piped unto you, and ye have not danced; we have mourned unto you, and ye have not lamented." There's no pleasing some of them, and it is rather depressing to know at the beginning of a performance, when I see a certain critic there, that even if I sing particularly well in a work that suits me perfectly the most I can expect is to be ignored, while the other soloists will be mentioned. If I am mentioned, it will be in a derogatory way. Now, I find myself especially vulnerable, not in any musical or artistic sense, but because of my type of voice, and it is something to which no other professional singer, to my knowledge, has been subjected. For instance, the eminent critic of one of our national daily newspapers, in writing up a performance of the Monteverdi Vespers at the Festival Hall, said something to the effect that "The soloists included the countertenor Alfred Deller. This voice can best be described as the soulmate to Mr Hoffnung's tuba." That may be funny, or it may not; but it can only be considered in the context of humour, and playing for cheap laughs. It has no value as music criticism at all, and yet it is the remark of a professional critic.

'As might be imagined, I realized long ago that I must expect an immediate reaction of shock when I began to sing to people who had never heard me before. I have trained myself not to be upset by it, and I only hope that the audience will quickly get over this natural surprise and settle down to listen to the voice as a musical instrument, and forget about me. Thank heaven, most people do. My worst moments, I'm sorry to say, have come from professional musicians in the larger orchestras when I have appeared in more orthodox concerts. After a rehearsal at Liverpool once I heard the principal of one of the wood-wind sections, a first-class player who might have been expected to know better, remark loudly to a colleague, "If my mother heard me sing like that in public, she'd disown me." And at the Festival Hall one night, as I stood in the wings waiting to begin an important concert, the leader of the famous orchestra turned to the eminent conductor and said, for me to hear, "I see we have the bearded lady with us tonight." What a charming way to begin a performance!

'I know perfectly well that what is involved here is an extra-musical consideration, arising from a quite pathetic notion of what constitutes a true man. If manliness is to mean toughness and virility, I can only suggest that the Elizabethans who used my type of voice and regarded it as altogether manly were a good deal tougher and more virile than most men today. I am a great big fellow of six foot two, and over fourteen stone; I'm the father of three; I've been a representative footballer and cricketer in my day, and I was the son of a professional gymnast: and yet, because I sing in a type of voice which has scarcely been heard for one hundred and fifty years, I can expect to be regarded as something less than a true man.

'In any case, my notion of true manhood has nothing whatever to do with these attributes of so-called toughness. A true man is someone whose whole mind and emotions are informed, and constantly being informed, so that through their exercise and the interplay between his intellect and emotions his personality develops, then his tastes and discrimination. This is nothing to do with the debased image of manhood which is constantly being thrust at us today.'

Deller's awareness that he is treading something of a

lonely path upon the heights has intensified an inherited feeling of being something of an outsider. 'All the Dellers have it,' says one who married into the family and has remained objective. 'There's a strong streak of detachment running through them, as if they're afraid to get too close to anyone else mentally. They're like it amongst themselves and with others. I think the lack of apparent warmth of affection in the family home made them tend to withdraw into themselves; but I also wonder, and I believe some of them have wondered, whether there is not some racial mixture in the past which might help to account for it. It might explain their exceptional darkness of hair and eyes, and some of Alfred's more mystical characteristics.'

Deller agrees. 'I have always felt a bit of an outsider. Even locally, where I have been living for years, I'm always conscious of being held at arm's length by people with whom I have daily contact. I can honestly say that I try to be natural and friendly, and talk about things they want to talk about; but I never quite get through. They always seem to me to be thinking, "This chap's an odd bod. He's not one of us." Some friends might guffaw to hear me say it, but I am basically extremely shy, added to which, I expect, I'm automatically on the defensive for prejudice, through misunderstanding, against my voice.'

Few great artists enjoy complete *rapport* with other beings, however close they may move from time to time, and Deller is no exception. A gap which possibly will never be bridged yawns between his good intentions and his ability to fulfil them, with the result that he is sometimes referred to as 'upstage' or 'a bit of a snob'. Neither accusation is true, though it is not hard to understand them. On the one hand stands the natural mystic, who admits to having toyed in his youth with the notion of joining a withdrawn religious order, but knows full well that he would have been seeking a dispensation and release after a few weeks; on the other, a totally dedicated artist, who will talk entrancingly and eloquently for hours about music and numerous other subjects, yet despite brave and often delightfully successful attempts to join in on less elevated planes of discussion will eventually lapse into silent half-attention. Success has changed him not at all, insist all who have known him from the days of obscurity; but Michael Tippett believes that, in another sense, it has:

'I think Alfred belongs in the tradition of religious lyricism, which is a very real tradition, and very deep in all our own English histories. You get a great quality from this, but you pay a price, which is that you get detached from a lot that happens in modern society: you go into a fortress of some kind. This may be your strength, of course; in any case, you have to live it out, you can't change it. But Alfred, in addition, has been drawn into this world of Renaissance and polyphonic music, and I've noticed, not only in him but in many people, that it becomes increasingly difficult for them to find its equivalent in the modern world, so they gradually withdraw.'

Deller replies, 'I would deny this most emphatically. Firstly, where music itself is concerned, my interests are by no means confined to the periods from which my repertoire is drawn. From the days of my youth in Hastings, when I used to attend every Friday night symphony concert, at sixpence a time, I've enjoyed all kinds of classical music. I love to hear the great masterpieces of symphonic writing—by some composers more than others, of course—and I can come as close to modern times as Stravinsky and Bartók, yes, and Britten and Tippett. Where I do stop, I'm afraid, is when I reach the writers of serial music. I have no point of contact with them. Music and art, for me, must have a relationship with the human condition as I understand it; and while I can accept highly intellectual exercises in form and counterpoint, such as Bach's, I find this modern form a mere series of notes, unrelated to anything, least of all to my emotions, my heart, my soul. The gap between it and me is too great. Sticking out my neck, perhaps, I suggest that more people who find this music unrewarding should say so honestly. I don't think there is anything to be gained, either by the public or by the composer, by merely pursuing the convention of being "with it" and supporting things which one really finds pointless.

'In this same way, I'm appalled to find bishops and other people who should know better going out of their way to encourage these "beat" groups, because they think it will please the kids. I like traditional jazz in small doses, and I quite like some modern jazz; but I loathe this beat music. I think it is an abomination, like the most outlandish examples of *avant garde* serial music, and I think it is highly dangerous from a human and sociological point of view. When I look at pictures of frenzied young people being "sent" I've no doubt at all that they're being got at by that same Old Nick who's been "sending" people since time immemorial. What the beat groups are doing is making incredible amounts of money for doing the Devil's work. I'm convinced that the whole question of dope-taking and juvenile delinquency is all linked with this rotten influence.

'As to those people who defend beat music by finding interesting traces of Gregorian chant, and so forth, in it, I believe they're talking absolute rot. You can take any music and find traces of other music in it; but it is what is made of those influences, what comes out at the other end, that matters, and what comes out in this case is an abomination.

'What I feel most strongly about, though, is the use of beat music in churches, in the liturgy. I think this is an utter mistake. There may be, in spite of what I think about it, a place for the use of beat music in the evangelization of young people in youth clubs, and other such places. But we have been told that the liturgy demands the best that we can offer—the *best*. We surround God with what we know to be the best in music, in painting, in light, in colour; and I do not believe for one moment that the adaptation to this debased form of music is the best we can offer. I hasten to admit that we've offered a lot of base music in the past in our liturgy—Victorian music particularly; but it has been done, however mistakenly, from the right motive, and in the way of a genuine impulse. I see beat Masses, and so on, as a cheap and deliberate device for luring young people into empty churches.'

His concern for the church which has had so strong an influence on his life remains deep, but he denies that he is a good Christian. 'I don't pray enough. I entertain too many doubts and fears which only get in because of weakness of faith; and I constantly tell myself that I should do more for people. I know I would never have made a monk, but I often wonder whether I might not have made a priest. I'm aware that what I have been able to do in music has given something to a lot of people. I tell myself that my work is a form of prayer, and a worthwhile act. Where I feel that I have failed is in not reaching the people who do not hear me sing. There are so many old and lonely people in this world, for instance. I tell myself that if I were to telephone the hospital and offer to visit them I should be doing something much more valuable. Of course, I can't, because I am always travelling or caught up in some other way, and there's very little left over outside my work; but the sense of failure is always with me. I feel that, apart from my music, I have not developed.'

He left the choir of St Paul's in the summer of 1962. He had been aware for some time that he was spending less time in the choir-stall than on the concert platform, and that there existed certain resentments amongst colleagues over his constant use of deputies in his cathedral work. A gentle push from Canon Collins launched him into full-time freelancing. He left St Paul's with much regret, perhaps sensing that he would be leaving behind more than the music of the church. His relationship with religion had owed much to emotion, had satisfied a large part of his emotional hunger. It saddened him to think that, from now on, he could expect that relationship to diminish more and more under the pressures of a career which, from its beginning, had owed the church so much. Still, when touring, he attends Mass whenever possible. He retains his link with St Paul's as a committee member of Christian Action, under the chairmanship of Canon Collins; but he rarely manages to attend meetings. His lessened contact with the church worries him, though it should not. The churchmen who have most influenced his life are unanimous in their opinion of the quality of his Christianity, and he is realist enough to know that he could not be other than what he is.

'To be brutally honest, I'm a one-track person, and that track is music. I can't conceive of life without it, and I would be a very depressing person to live with if it were taken away from me. No, there it is, and I am not a big enough person to change things now.'

The end of his association with St Paul's freed Deller at last to accept more of the engagements awaiting him outside Britain. He had made his first trip abroad—the first of his life for any purpose— in 1949, at the age of thirty-seven, to sing in Geneva. He had gone hesitantly: it was his first experience of flying also, and he declares that nothing less than so important an engagement would have persuaded him off the ground. He still dislikes air travel, suffering through perils quite unapparent to his fellow passengers: necessity, however, dictates that he fly increasing thousands of miles each year, leaping from country to country with barely a day's rest between taxing engagements. Frankly, he would prefer not to travel anywhere, ever. He appreciates none of its forms and spends as much of it as possible in sleep.

By trial and error the Consort have disciplined their travelling into a manageable routine. The first obstacle they can expect to encounter is Deller's propensity for scribbling dates, information and programmes on the backs of old envelopes (a hark-back to his poems to Peggy on lino tiles?). He does not employ any full-time professional manager to travel with them, but relies on agents in various countries to make all arrangements for travel and accommodation. At other times these chores fall upon his well-organized baritone, Maurice Bevan.

Desmond Dupré recalls that on their first American tour together Deller took an amount of baggage which could only be described as fantastic, including a suitcase full of bound music and another crammed with super-fluous clothes, both of which remained unopened in their agent's office in New York. Now, he carries the minimum possible. He hates leaving home and reacts by being distant and aloof for the preceding twenty-four hours. As soon as he is away, and his gastric juices have adjusted themselves satisfactorily to the time changes between countries, he is all right again. He has made no effort to learn foreign languages: he relies largely upon instinct to guide his interpretation of foreign music, and upon phonetics for singing it. He is not interested in sight-seeing or any of the other fringe compensations for enforced travel. He wishes only to do his job and to husband his physical and mental resources to enable him to do it with unflagging excellence, sleeping whenever opportunity permits and holding constant vigil over his digestion. At home, his tendency towards hypochondria manifests itself in rows of bottles in the bathroom cup-board, most of them natural tonics which he has embraced in turn for a time before discovering something more promising. On tour, he makes do with Entero-vioform, by which he swears. He can drink what he likes with impunity. He smokes a pipe, and sometimes cigarettes, but does not inhale. His throat only preoccupies him immediately before he is due to sing. Then, if he can convince himself that he is going to suffer a frog in the throat, he will begin clearing it over and over again until all his colleagues feel their throats becoming sore in sympathy. The throat-clearing continues on to the plat-form itself, sometimes to the dismay of the front row of the audience, and the Consort will hear a despairing groan issue from him as he surrenders to the certainty that his voice is about to seize up. The music begins, and his throat is forgotten.

Since all his tours are successful, he returns home elated, though exhausted. He and Peggy go out to a restaurant for a meal, over which he relates his experiences and gradually unwinds. The night's sleep is enough to restore his energy. After his continental-style breakfast, followed by a pipe while he does three or four clues in the newspaper crossword, he makes eagerly for the study where the accumulated post awaits him. Work, and the prospect of work, are his greatest revivers. The increased frequency of his tours seldom leaves him more than a few days at home, so there is little danger of his slipping into

153

that dangerous *ennui* which brings his vitality and spirits to their lowest ebb. He has no hobbies, and needs none. The total vulnerability of a one-track life preys often on his mind: he knows he is stuck with it, and no adopted pursuits could console him if he were deprived of it.

Peggy, who admits that she once begrudged him his opportunity to travel while domestic and economic necessity kept her confined to the home, has now come to terms with spending more than half of each year alone. When she can travel with him, she does. When she cannot, she finds the days all too short for her numerous activities. Of late, she has had more than enough to occupy her handling all the arrangements for buying and renovating the fourteenth-century farmhouse in Provence which has become their second home.

Mark is married and living at Salisbury, where he is a lay clerk at the cathedral. As a countertenor he emerges honourably from any comparison with his father. They often appear and tour together, and in 1966 Mark made his American debut with the Consort. His career has brought great gratification to Deller, who admits that he had scarcely allowed himself to hope that his son would share his experience of making the transition from promising boy singer to adult professional, least of all as a countertenor.

'When Mark went into The King's School, Canterbury, at fourteen,' he says, 'I thought that would be the moment for it all to end, which would have been natural enough. Instead, he identified himself with the school's music straight away, especially with the re-formed Madrigal Society, and, what is more, as an alto, though I had done nothing at all to push him into trying to sing across the break as I had done. In due course he wrote to tell us that he was going to try to get into Cambridge University as a choral scholar. He came and stayed overnight with us on his way to take his voice test. I asked him what the test piece was to be. He had chosen *Return, O God of hosts* from *Samson*. I sat down at the piano and said, "All right, I might as well hear it." He sang it through, and I remember making one or two observations, such as "I wouldn't breathe there", and so on. That was all the coaching he had ever had from me before taking that test and coming first out of more than twenty candidates.'

Mark Deller's voice resembles his father's closely in tone and quality, and, heard but not seen, it is almost impossible to pick out the difference between them in short passages. More prolonged listening reveals the sound to be smaller and paler, less ripe than his father's, which owes something to maturity. Like any other follower in Deller's footsteps he can scarcely hope to scale the same heights of eminence. Alfred Deller's voice and artistry are unlikely ever to be surpassed, and what remains of his 'novelty' as the reviver of a long-lost art must ensure him the edge over all future comers. Even so, Mark's quality is such that when the father does at last have to retire, his son may be expected to take his place and the Deller Consort continue to exist without any loss of its present matchless standard.

Mark taught for some time in the Salisbury choir school, working, like his father, on a farm for a while to augment his income. Following his father's other example of marrying the boss's daughter, he married Sheelagh

Benson, the daughter of his headmaster there. His interest in organizing concerts and musical groups at Canterbury and Cambridge remains with him. He has presented many performances of chamber, choral and orchestral works in the city's cathedral close and in the fine old Guildhall, and in 1966 was appointed Artistic Director of Salisbury's first Festival of the Arts.

While Mark Deller resembles his father in voice but neither in stature nor particularly in appearance, his younger brother Simon's inheritance has been the other way about. He is his father's height and build, and is a younger, beardless reflection of his image. He sings bass. His voice broke exceptionally early, forcing him to leave Canterbury Choir School. He did well academically at the City of London School, where he managed to keep up his interest in music, which he studied as first subject when he went on to Nottingham Teacher's Training College. He married a fellow student, Mollie Stallard, and is now a lay vicar at Ripon Cathedral and teaches in the choir school, where his headmaster is his father's former colleague in the choir of St Paul's Cathedral, the Rev. Duncan Thomson.

The other child, Jane, in whose pretty face the dark Deller eyes appear most strikingly of all, has her share of musical gifts and ambitions. She is a talented pianist, and at the time of writing, with her schooldays barely ended, is about to enter a teachers' training college, with Art as first subject.

As a parent, Deller is described by one of his family as 'perhaps a little distant'. Peggy recalls how, earlier in their marriage, it used to irritate her to hear him praising qualities in other people's children to which he was apprently oblivious in his own. For their part, the children have recognized the extent of the demands made upon his mental and physical stamina by his career, and have accepted any lack of intimacy without resentment. They have found ample compensation in their mother. There are frequent family reunions, which, if he does not fully demonstrate it, Deller enjoys as much as anyone in his rôle of slightly aloof patriarch. When relaxed and in the mood he has shared many hilarious times with the family, especially round the card table. Pontoon, for small stakes, has always been a favourite of them all. His Boy Scout's love of camping has never quite left him. When the children were small the family would go on camping holidays to Scotland and the Norfolk Broads. Gradually, Deller's propensity for roughing it decreased, and an essential feature of their equipment came to be 'a table and chair for father'. Every spring since moving to Barton Cottage he has been heard to declare his intention of taking a small bivouac tent on to the Wye Downs for a few nights. He has never done so, and knows he never will; but the mystique of the open air remains a potent thing for him.

As man about the house he is incompetent, knows it, and has no intention of trying to reform. Anything mechanical defeats him utterly. It is useless for Peggy to seek his help in removing an obstinate electric light bulb from its socket, or screwing a fitting into a wall. After a cursory glance he will declare the project impossible, and wander away, leaving her to get on with it herself. When the problem is abstract, rather than practical, it is a different matter. He has always been a willing listener to people's problems and seldom at a loss for advice to offer, a manifestation of the priest *manqué*, which Peggy, who has seen more of it than anyone, regards as suspect.

'It worries me at times, because people so readily accept what he tells them,' she says. 'He has a gift with words, and a remarkable memory for anything he's read, so that he can very easily produce a quotation which seems to fit the case, but doesn't really, if you stop to think about it. People go away thinking he's a marvel of wisdom: then they come back for more, and perhaps find that he's lost all interest. He has helped a lot of people in very practical ways: but generally he can't keep it up, with the result that I'm sometimes left to try to cope with their problems where he dropped them.'

Again and again with Alfred Deller, the same cause and effect are seen. His whole thought and energy are focussed upon his career. Little remains for externals, though, occasionally, good intentions flare up, burn briefly, then are snuffed out abruptly as the main demand reasserts itself. This is one reason why he has done comparatively little in the way of teaching. Many young men aspiring to become countertenors apply to him for a course of lessons, and he helps them when he feels able. He also advises a number of professional singers of various voices on questions of interpretation of works in which they are to take part. In teaching, as in performing, though, he tends to commit himself totally, emotions and all, and the strain is too great. He was flattered some years ago to be invited by Keith Faulkner, Principal of the Royal College of Music, to join the staff and teach the countertenor voice; but, wisely, he declined. One appointment he did accept was as visiting professor to the Rheinische Schule für alte Musik, Cologne, which involves regular brief visits. He devotes a little time each year to advising the University of Kent, Canterbury, on its occasional concerts, which he sometimes conducts; and in the course of his own tours, especially of the United States, he generally manages to work in brief seminars at universities at which he is performing.* Otherwise, there is neither the time nor the energy for teaching. Those who wish to learn from him must do so by hearing him perform, either in person or through the media of radio or recordings.

Although his career owes much to radio, notably from the early years of the B.B.C. Third Programme, Deller is by no means as frequent a broadcaster today as might be wished, though not from any unwillingness on his

---

* He accepted the University of Kentucky's invitation to fill the Bingham Chair of Humanities for the spring semester of 1968, the first musician to be so honoured.

part. He has, however, made many recordings, almost all of which are of a technical excellence worthy of his art. Ironically, the majority of them are almost unknown and unobtainable in his own country.* After making his first, 78 r.p.m. discs for H.M.V., he was approached by the Dutch harpsichordist Gustav Leonhardt, then teaching at the Vienna Conservatoire, who had been asked by the Vanguard Recording Society Inc. of New York to make recordings of Bach cantatas and Elizabethan and Jacobean music with a vocal ensemble. Would Deller care to take part in these recordings? He would be delighted: and Vanguard, delighted with the results, offered him an exclusive contract. H.M.V. released him, and the consequence has been that almost all his own and the Consort's considerable recording activity for more than a decade has been under the aegis of Vanguard's Bach Guild label. These superb recordings, which have afforded him immense scope of repertoire and have brought him into association with many of the world's leading instrumental ensembles specializing in his periods of music, have made him familiar to American and European music-lovers. Because Vanguard recordings are not distributed in Great Britain, his exclusive contract with them has kept him correspondingly little appreciated here. It represents his one constant professional disappointment; and it is at last being overcome. In 1966, he at last terminated the Vanguard contract in order to join Bernard Coutaz, of the French Harmonia Mundi recording company, in founding Alfred Deller Recordings, for which he and the Consort now record almost exclusively. Their recordings have world-wide distribution, and have been acclaimed wherever they have been heard, including countries where Deller has never appeared in person and the music of Purcell, Dowland and Campion has hitherto been unknown.

Like many artists, Deller enjoys a love-hate relation-

---

* For complete Discography, *see* p. 181.

ship with recording. He dislikes the tyranny of technical demands and the financial necessity of getting through the maximum amount of work in the minimum time. He refuses to indulge in the modern practice of assembling a clinically perfect performance by constant re-taking and editing-in of passages which have not been one hundred per cent; though he will edit where a distinct flaw is noticeable. He will not subscribe to the other extreme, what he describes as 'Let's all be jolly together—hit or miss, so long as we get the spirit of the thing'. This he regards as the amateur approach. He dislikes the inescapable long periods of waiting about in the recording studio, listening to other artists doing their part and then having to get up 'cold' to the microphone to do his. Constant stops for technical reasons and to listen to playbacks destroy the continuity of the work for him. Experience, however, has taught him to overcome these inhibitions and to feel in the recording studio that he is singing before a perfectly mannered and warmly responsive concert audience.

Again, like many colleagues, he is critical of his early recordings; not of the quality of his and the Consort's performances, but of what he sees as a certain inhibition of style, for which he is inclined to blame the technical side of things. 'I realize when I play one of those early recordings how much faster and more assured we are today in performing, say, English madrigals,' he admits. 'Everything is there, but too carefully done. With my lack of experience at the time, I must have let my natural instinct for tempi be moderated by what I thought was the vital necessity to have every part heard distinctly. So everything was taken a little stodgily, whereas today we perform those same works quite differently and much quicker, and yet without losing a thing.' For all his reservations, he is conscious of his great debt to recording and to the mysteriously gifted technicians who have joined their skill with his to produce the discs which have multiplied his world audience countless times over.

Much of his recording now, for his own company, takes place in the tiny church of All Saints, Boughton Aluph, which has stood since the thirteenth century in the rural peace of the Stour Valley, only a few miles from the rapidly-growing town of Ashford and Deller's own house. He first became aware of the remarkable acoustical properties of the remote little church when his artist friend, John Ward, R.A., also a resident in the Stour Valley, persuaded him to have a look at the superbly proportioned fourteenth-century workmanship of the interior. Deller did more than look: he sang a few bars. The acoustics astonished him. But it was not until something like a year later that he suddenly remarked, during tea on the front porch of his home, 'Wouldn't it be marvellous if we could have some music in that church?' It was the beginning of what has since been an annual event attended by music lovers from many countries, as well as from the county of Kent—Stour Music.

The first of these delightfully intimate festivals was held in 1963, and lasted one day. Deller and other artists took part in a concert in Boughton Aluph church, and the Philomusica Orchestra, with the Deller Consort as soloists and a choir drawn from many parts of the county,

performed a Bach programme, including the Magnificat
in D, in the parish church of one of the Stour Valley's,
and England's, most attractive villages, Chilham, and
an evening concert in the evocatively atmospheric setting
of Olantigh, the stately Stour Valley home of Mr William
and Lady Prudence Loudon. The following year the
festival lasted three days. The Olantigh concert was sold
out, and has been at every Stour Music since, while most
of the other events are attended by capacity, or near-
capacity audiences. Besides Deller and the Consort,
artists of the first rank enable Stour Music to reflect the
late John Christie's expressed aim for Glyndebourne:
'Not the best we can do, but the best that can be done
anywhere.' It is impossible to conceive any more satisfying musical occasion than, for instance, a performance
at Olantigh of a Purcell work by the Deller Consort and
the contemporary instruments of the Concentus Musicus
of Vienna, with a Cordon Bleu buffet in the interval and
an informal mingling of artists and audience over drinks
in the Old Brewhouse afterwards.

Above all his foreign triumphs, Deller regards Stour Music as the high spot of his year. Fortunately for its survival, perhaps, the organization is handled not by him, but by a committee, with a paragon of a secretary, a retired Civil Servant with no previous musical background, George Dracup. But it is Deller's enthusiasm that colours the whole affair, and their respect for him that persuades artists to travel from abroad to perform for small fees and consider it a privilege to do so. The heroine of the entire venture is Peggy Deller. Throughout the festival period her life and home are completely disrupted. All members of the family are turned from their beds in order to give accommodation to visiting artists. Those performers who cannot be housed at Barton Cottage are put up in other people's houses, but many of them descend on Peggy for their meals. A large marquee in the garden houses a running buffet of food and wine for artists and important guests, all catered for and run by Peggy and devoted non-professional helpers.

Stour Music is no different from most music festivals in failing to meet its costs, although Deller was able to tell a recent audience that what had been a sizeable overdraft the year before had been reduced to 'a manageable deficit —which in these days is riches indeed'. The fact is that with most of its audiences at capacity level the festival can look forward to little more income than it now attracts, but must inevitably face rising costs. To extend it in scope would be to make it something it never set out to be and to sacrifice the essential intimacy which makes it a unique musical experience. While he is confident of the festival's future, Deller continues to hope for a modern Maecenas to emerge. Those who organize and perform in Stour Music are doing their utmost to keep it what it is: any further act of faith in it will have to come from its audiences and well-wishers.

In the four days of Stour Music Deller himself is more seen than heard. He conducts more than he sings (discounting his habit of singing all the parts of any work he happens to be conducting, against which members of the Consort have been known to retaliate by chipping in on his part when next he has legitimately sung with them). He has no wish to be guilty of self-aggrandizement through 'his' festival, and so tends to appear less as a soloist than some members of his audiences would wish. There is no question of any deliberate easing off, now that he has reached an age when most singers' voices are past their prime. He has always recognized the need to husband his voice, like his energy. The creation of the Consort has enabled him to do this, while also permitting him to make sparing use of a not extensive solo repertoire. Perhaps where his top comfortable note was once E it is now D. Perhaps the 'Dellerism' of shading a high note down to *pianissimo* is sometimes now resorted to as an

TWELVE

A CONVERSATION WITH DELLER

lfred Deller's is so personal an art, and he
expresses his views upon it so fluently in conversation, that we feel that the reader might care to
have, in Deller's own words, his answers to certain
questions we put to him.

Picture him, one morning, in the heavily beamed
drawing-room of Barton Cottage. A small log fire smokes
idly in the vastness of the inglenook fireplace, contributing
only atmosphere to the electrically heated room. Beside it,
Deller inhabits his tall winged chair, his back to the
window, the bearded face dark-shaded from the light.
He wears a flame-coloured woollen cardigan of uncertain
age which Peggy has tried unsuccessfully many times over
the years to wrest from his possession and quietly lose. A
large thermos jug of good coffee stands on the table
beside him, most of it destined to waste. After one cup,
Deller will be too deep in conversation to remember to
pour more, either for himself or for his interviewers. One
helps oneself while he talks on, occasionally pausing to
light his pipe but too occupied to keep it going.

Four cats are distributed about the room. The ancient

Siamese, Yung, invests one interviewer's lap, Katie the other's. The kittens Henry and Sophocles (formerly Sophie, until someone found out) embrace and dream in the hearth. None of them ever sits on Deller's lap.

The distant sounds of the household mingle with the buzz of traffic on the busy road just beyond the hedge of the ancient garden. Without pausing to take thought in answer to any question, leaning forward to emphasize every point, grimacing and raising his eyebrows as far as they will go to express any form of outrage or wonderment, Alfred Deller talks.

DELLER: There's a widely held opinion that the countertenor is an essentially English voice. This isn't true. It was, in fact, a European voice. There is a good deal of evidence to support the view that if it is not the oldest known voice type, it is *one* of the oldest; and we find composers in several countries writing for it as far back as the thirteenth century, in ensemble and as a solo voice. Later, of course, Bach employed not only *castrati*, but countertenors, descant singers. Mind you, having said that, there's no doubt that England was the place where the voice was especially widely used and developed, particularly in the seventeenth century.

Q: But do you feel justified in singing Bach's alto arias? Are they really suited to the countertenor voice?

DELLER: The quick answer to that is that Bach would certainly have used boys, or students, never women; therefore, historically speaking, I don't see that there can be any objection. Then, I feel, the question of pitch becomes very relevant here. To be absolutely frank, as things are with the modern pitch, most of the Bach arias lie uncomfortably high for the countertenor. If we wish to hear the B minor Mass as Bach heard it we must perform it in A minor, at least a whole tone lower, because pitch has been going up and up since about 1860.

Q: Then, works which could be in your repertoire—and should be, historically speaking—have been taken out of your range by the rise in pitch?

DELLER: Yes. If the pitch were lowered by a whole tone, everything that Bach wrote for the alto would be comfortably within my range. As it is, I can, and do, perform single arias out of context, because they can be transposed. For example, one of the first recordings I made for Vanguard, more or less as a fill-up, was the *Agnus Dei* from the B minor Mass. I've had letters from many parts of the world from people saying that this has given them a completely new conception of Bach. I think this is because of the particular ability of the countertenor voice to convey the religious sense of the work, and from the instrumental quality of the voice, especially in a slow-moving aria. I remember Michael Tippett remarking on this when we first did the Bach Magnificat. There's a marvellous duet for alto and tenor, *Et Misericordia*; but you see, it's highish in the tenor and quite low for the contralto, and there is a problem to get a real matching. When the voices go one above the other and sometimes the alto goes below the tenor, then it's not a question of whether the contralto is any good, or not, but whether you can really get this intertwining of sounds and timbre between the two voices. With the countertenor replacing the alto you really can get it, because of this instrumental quality I'm speaking of. Out of the same work there's the *Esurientis* for alto, which pipes along with two flutes. The countertenor voice, having this same sort of fluty sound, answers the instruments ideally, while a female voice, however beautiful its quality, just doesn't match the quality of the instruments.

Q: Does the repertoire available to you fulfil all your needs?

DELLER: I think the whole literature from, shall we say, the thirteenth century right through to Bach and

Handel offers music in plenty to express everything that I might wish to express. As to the nineteenth century, I've been absolutely firm since I started to sing as a professional to keep clear of all the composers of the romantic period, except for my own pleasure. They didn't conceive their music for anything like my type of voice, and it can never make their songs sound right. I love Schubert's songs, and when I was eighteen I won the *lieder* classes of two musical festivals in Kent with *Du bist die Ruh*. But I only did it because there was no special category for my kind of voice, and it was a case of sing Schubert or don't enter at all.

Q: But you have been prepared to perform works by modern composers who have written for you?

DELLER: Certainly. I'm interested that music should be written by contemporary composers for the countertenor voice, and I think it is possible to achieve good results. The obvious example is the marvellous part Britten wrote for me in *A Midsummer Night's Dream*. I have also sung interesting works in the modern idiom written for me by people like Michael Tippett, Edmund Rubbra, Wilfrid Mellers and Racine Fricker.

Q: In performing works of the thirteenth to seventeenth centuries, say, aren't you up against some difficulties not only of pitch, but of matching your voice to modern instruments?

DELLER: Very much so. Not only have most modern instrumentalists no conception of how to play down sufficiently to get a real sense of ensemble, but their instruments make it almost impossible to get a convincing balance. The works were simply not conceived for, shall we say, modern violins using wire strings and sound posts here and there to get the utmost resonance out of the instrument. Therefore, whenever the Consort records a major work, we try to ensure that it is in association with someone like the Concentus Musicus of Vienna, using original

instruments. Then the whole thing takes on an entirely different aspect. There is no question here of trying to create atmosphere for its own sake, or achieve 'period' effects. The old instruments, by their very nature and size, and the fact that they have gut strings, and so on, can play with a convincing vitality of sound which really matches the voice. Moreover, they can do this and still play softly enough in an alto aria such as *A refiner's fire* in the *Messiah*, which a modern orchestra, however sympathetic, cannot play without losing that vitality. As another example, when we performed the *Messiah* in the 1966 Stour Music with the Concentus Musicus, Maurice Bevan sang *The trumpet shall sound* not with a modern trumpet, but with a clarino, and there's no other word than ethereal for the result. Naturally, when your baritone sings that aria with a modern trumpet he feels he has to give his all to match the trumpet's sound. Now, at the first rehearsal, when we heard the clarino I said to Maurice, 'This is what Handel meant! "The trumpet shall sound"—not the martial sound of the military trumpet, on a human level of calling the forces together, but as a heavenly trumpet from afar, the still, small trumpet in the ear.' Maurice scaled down his performance accordingly; he didn't have to struggle at all, and the whole thing was a revelation.

Q: Surely, the ideal would be for the Deller Consort to have its own instrumental ensemble, with original instruments, working with it constantly in mutual understanding?

DELLER: Vocally, that is exactly why I formed the Consort. As to instrumentalists, nothing would give me greater delight, for example, than to get up here in the morning at Barton Cottage, eat a leisurely breakfast, then be able to say, 'Right, ladies and gentlemen, we'll work for an hour or two before lunch . . . .' If one had all the money in the world, it would be quite easy to contrive, and it would be possible to make ideal performances of many wonderful works which the normal rush of engagements doesn't make it possible to study and rehearse. But money and organizational problems rule this out, and it isn't possible to team up, as it were, with any one existing instrumental ensemble, because all of them, like us, have their own engagements and travelling which would conflict too much. Fortunately, instead, we've been able to work on the Continent with such wonderful ensembles as the Scuola Cantorum Basiliensis, of Basle, the Capella Colloniensis, of Cologne, the Musica Antiqua, of Vienna, and, of course, the Concentus Musicus. In America, a lot of universities have extremely good collegium ensembles, with whom it's a pleasure to work.

Q: Is there an ideal accompaniment to your own voice?

DELLER: I think I enjoy singing to the lute more than anything else, not only because of the quality of its sound but because I have suffered so much from trying to get a balance when having to sing with any other instrument that has happened to be available.*

Q: Similarly, are there ideal performance conditions?

DELLER: Thank God, nothing takes the place of public performances. Believe me, it isn't just a question of wanting applause—though, of course, it's always pleasurable to hear lots of it and know that one is going across well. But for me, particularly, the music of the Renaissance, and so on, represents a sort of conversation between the artist and the audience. You've got to establish a *rapport* between you, and get to know one another quickly in order to do full justice to the music as artist and hearer. I would say that one knows, as an artist, within the first few minutes of beginning to perform whether that *rapport* exists already, or can be achieved by working at it, or won't be forthcoming at all. Generally, of course, a fairly small audience in intimate surroundings gives one the best chance. I reckon six or seven hundred, given the right hall and the right acoustic, is about ideal. But whether one is performing to a couple of hundred at Olantigh, or a couple of thousand in a town hall, it's the acoustic which really matters. For vocal ensemble music, we like it to be lively, not too dry—something with a bit of resonance. I've said something small with a few hundred people is ideal, but we've had some surprises in our travels. I think of that vast hall in the University of Iowa, which must seat two thousand comfortably, where Desmond Dupré, Robert Conant and I performed some years ago, just raised on a

---

* Desmond Dupré says, 'A harpsichord is perfectly all right for slightly later works, and I think the voice and the instrument go together well. I think the lute has the advantage that the countertenor voice, certainly as used by Alfred, goes in more than any other for a lot of dynamic change, a great many dynamic nuances, which you can't get on a harpsichord satisfactorily. A piano can do it, but that doesn't really suit the voice, whereas a lute can do it and does suit the voice.'

platform in this vast arena—and they said every single note was audible at the back. Then there's the Sydney Town Hall. It seems as big as Euston Station when you've got to sing in it. We had an audience of eighteen hundred and I believe they heard every note.

Q: You're sensitive about the way you're treated after the performance, as well as during it. Is there an ideal form of hospitality which concert organizers might do well to copy?

DELLER: Artists vary, of course, but for my part, and the Consort's—and I think a lot of others would agree—the immediate need is to unwind a bit, to recover. You can't do this if you're thrust into the middle of a throng, even if it's an admiring one, and expected to meet people and talk. What we like best is to be shown to a table in some other room at which we can sit down and have a few quiet drinks and something to eat. Then one joins the party afterwards feeling fully able to do so, and I think both sides get more pleasure from it as a result.

Q: You've been speaking of the ordinary listener's response to you: now, what about the professionals in the audience—the critics, the musicologists? Does their presence inhibit you at all?

DELLER: It used to a little, but not now. One can only do one's best as one conceives it, and hope to be criticized without prejudice. As to musicologists, well, I tend to think of them as inhabiting two distinct worlds. There are those whose work I accept and appreciate—the ones who have done so much, particularly in recent years, to rediscover manuscripts and writings on music which have been extremely valuable to the practising musician. But there are the others who enter the realm of practical music, and then it can be very dangerous. To write intelligently on a musical subject—even, if you like, to discuss what pertains in the way of notation and

give their views about stylistic indications—is one thing. To come between artists and their art is another. The tendency is to drain the music of any inherent life, and produce the type of performance which they refer to on the Continent as 'vegetarian music'. A German performer told me once that before the first rehearsal of a major Bach work in Munich the conductor addressed them all to the effect that, 'We want no sense of emotion in this work at all.' Now, this is something I've been up against with musicologists myself. The basic thing with me, all the time, is that even if music was written four hundred years ago it was written by human beings for human beings; and human beings have not changed in their fundamental hungers, and desires, and emotions. Ninety per cent of the madrigal texts, for instance, are on the subject of unrequited love or on the joys of love fulfilled. In my opinion it is absolute nonsense to treat these marvellous works coldly: in which case, however beautifully they are played and sung, there will be no real personal communication through them. Unfortunately, these people who would de-vitalize such works are nothing if not industrious, and write for every possible publication, so that they have managed to influence for the worse the performance by well-meaning amateurs, if not by professionals, of a great deal of old music. No, I think musicology and the performance of music are two worlds best kept apart from one another.

Q: Apart from 'beware of musicologists!', have you any other advice for aspiring countertenors—indeed, for other singers?

DELLER: An important thing for a countertenor to bear in mind always is that there's nothing remarkable about being able to sing high. A lot of men can sing higher than I can. What matters is what one does with the voice, how one uses it, and this is something which cannot really be taught to anyone who can't experience it instinctively. There's a constant mistake on the part of young, enthusiastic countertenors to attempt things which are unnecessarily high, or, even when they're at liberty to transpose, to choose to sing at too high a *tessitura*. From the point of view of mechanics alone the voice must thin out as it goes higher, however well the notes are negotiated, so that there isn't the possibility of getting real resonance. Young singers say to me, 'Of course, in the morning I can take a top A', as though I am supposed to fall over backwards in admiration. I hasten to point out that it isn't necessary at all:

if they would put their songs down lower, they would develop much more resonance in the voice.

The most important thing for all singers, I believe, is an understanding, and an acceptance, and a humility in the presence of what Nature has given you. As I see it, in providing you with a voice of one type or another, Nature has given you a frame of certain dimensions. You've been handed the frame: now, you have to fill in the space it encloses; and you achieve much of this by hard work. But, by the mystery of God, every voice, even a great voice, has been given a frame of specific dimensions, and there's nothing to be gained by trying to alter it. It's no use saying, 'I'm a lyric tenor, but I'm going to become a dramatic tenor, because I want to sing Wagner.' I'm afraid this does happen. There are those sopranos with beautiful mezzo voices, straining away at trying to become dramatic opera singers until their voices become shrill and full of vibrato and out of context. Unless one faces up to making the most of what one has been given, and not trying to kick against the pricks, one won't achieve anything. This applies perhaps even more so to counter-tenors, who should, in my opinion, be very careful to confine themselves to the music written for the voice and not try to embark on things which were never intended for the male alto to sing.

Q: You have filled in the frame of your art as fully as one can conceive of its being done. Yet, you seem to feel that if life, like art, has its God-given frame, you have somehow failed to fill yours completely. What more do you think you could possibly have done?

DELLER: I think, as I said, that there has been something lacking in the way of human relationships; though, in my defence, I must repeat that this has sprung from what is basically a deep shyness on my part which some people have read incorrectly as a sense of my own superiority and importance. We're all guilty of this too often in life. We meet someone and too easily form some impression of them, come to a conclusion about them, and only when we get to know them really well do we find it completely disproved. One of the most important things in our relationship with our fellow beings seems to me to be to remember that things are seldom what they seem in any of us. My other fundamental regret, perhaps, is this feeling of not having done enough for those people whom my art doesn't reach.

Q: This feeling that you should be visiting the sick, and so forth: to be honest, if you had the leisure, would you really do it?

DELLER: I'm afraid not. I know that I am one of those one-track people, and that my life is music and nothing outside of it.

Q: In saying that, are you perhaps indulging in a convenient kind of escapism—using it as a good excuse for not facing up to the bigger issues?

DELLER: I may be. But, genuinely, for good or ill, music is the one thing in my life. Perhaps if music had left me, and I'd been given the leisure you speak of, I might have managed to do something with it. But I can't conceive of that. I can't conceive of life without music, and I believe that, if it did stop, I would be unable to do anything else. It's the one thing that gives meaning to my existence—my work, my music. Everything stems from it. Everything.

The following is a complete list of the seventy-two albums and individual discs in which Alfred Deller participates as singer, conductor, or both. The nationality of each of the five recording companies concerned does not, of course, imply that the recordings are available only in the respective countries; but, unfortunately, the majority of those of foreign origin are not readily available in Great Britain and need determined tracking down through the specialist dealers. The quest is well worth the necessary effort and patience.

Decca (Great Britain)

SOSARME (Handel)—Complete recording (6 sides)—with full cast and orchestra cond. Anthony Lewis   OL 50091–3

MAGNIFICAT IN D MAJOR (Bach), 2 sides—with other soloists and St Anthony Singers cond. Pierre Colombo.   OL 50101

LUTENIST SONGS: *Never Weatherbeaten Sail* (Campion); *Most Sweet and Pleasing are Thy Ways, O God* (Campion); *Author of Light* (Campion); *Fantasia* (Milano)—Lute solo; *To Music Bent* (Campion); *Miserere My Maker* (anon., *c.* 1615)—with Desmond Dupré (Lute), Buxtehude: *Jubilate Domino*—Cantata for solo voice; *Fugue in C Major* —Organ solo; *In Dulci Jubilo*— Cantata for three voices—with Eileen McLoughlin (Sop.) and Maurice Bevan (Bass); Instrumentalists: Goren and Friedman

(Violins); Shuttleworth (Cello); Desmond Dupré (Viola da Gamba) and Vaughan (Organ). OL 50102

COME YE SONS OF ART (Purcell). *Miserere* (Lully)—with other soloists and St Anthony Singers cond. Lewis. OL 50166

MISERERE (Lully), 2 sides— with other soloists and St Anthony Singers cond. Lewis. DL 53003
(deleted)

COME YE SONS OF ART (Purcell), 2 sides—with other soloists and St Anthony Singers cond. Lewis. DL 53004
(deleted)

A MIDSUMMER NIGHT'S DREAM (Britten)—Complete recording (6 sides)—with full cast and orchestra cond. Benjamin Britten, assisted by Stuart Bedford. SET 338–40
MET 338–40

H.M.V. (Great Britain)
SHAKESPEARE SONGS AND LUTE SOLOS—with Desmond Dupré (Lute). ALP 1265

Deller Recordings (Great Britain in association with Harmonia Mundi (France))
JOHN BLOW. *Ode on the death of Purcell, and Marriage ode.* With Deller Consort, Walter Bergmann (Harpsichord) and Stour Festival Chamber Orchestra. DR 201

SHAKESPEARE SONGS. With Desmond Dupré (Lute) and Deller Consort. DR 202

GESUALDO. *Sacrae Cantiones, and Madrigals*. With Deller Consort. DR 203

'CONSORTIANA'. *English, French and Italian music of the Renaissance*. With Deller Consort. DR 204

ENGLISH MADRIGALS AND SONGS. With Deller Consort. DR 205

MUSIC FOR CHRISTMAS. *Carl Orff Instrumentarium*. With Deller Consort, choir of girls from Ashford, instrumental ensemble cond. Bergmann. DR 206

HENRY PURCELL. *Te Deum and Jubilate Deo in D major. In Guilty Night (Saul and the Witch of Endor). Man that is born of woman (Funeral Sentences)*. With Deller Consort, Stour Music Festival Choir, Orchestra, instrumentalists and chamber organ cond. Deller. DR 207

THOMAS TALLIS. *The Lamentations of Jeremiah the Prophet. Hymns with plainsong and polyphony*. With Deller Consort and chamber organ. DR 208

MONTEVERDI. *Tirsi e Clori* (Ballo concertato con voci e strumenti a cinque); *Hor' Ch'el e la Terra* (part II), Madrigal a 6 con 2 violini e basso; *Madrigals*. With Deller Consort and Collegium Aureum ensemble. DR 209

FRANCOIS COUPERIN. *Leçons de Ténèbres (pour le Mercredy Saint).* With Philip Todd (tenor), organ and viola da gamba.   DR 210

Harmonia Mundi (Germany)
DIE   SEEMANNSBRAUT. *Seeabenteuer, Segelschiffe. Matrosenlieder auf Schallplatte.* With Deller Consort.   HM 17070

PRIMAVERA. *Novellen, Gedichte und Gestalten der Frührenaissance. Madrigal und Tanzmusik auf Schallplatte. Tänze aus 'Musique de Joye'* (Jacques Moderne), *'Zefiro torna'* (Monteverdi). With Deller Consort and instrumentalists.   HM 17068

MITTELALTERLICHE WEIHNACHT. *Viderunt omnes* (Perotinus Magnus), *Maria zart* (Arnolt Schlick). With Elly Ameling (Sop.), Deller Consort and instrumentalists.   HM 17016

MUSIK AN NOTRE DAME IN PARIS UM 1200. With Deller Consort and instrumentalists.   HMS 30 823

ORAZIO VECCHI. *L'Amfiparnaso.* With Deller Consort and instrumentalists.   HM 30 628–9

GUILLAUME DE MACHAUT. *Messe Nostre Dame.* With Deller Consort and instrumentalists.   HM 25 148

Vanguard (U.S.A.)
FOLK SONGS, CAROLS AND FAVOURITE SONGS
THE THREE RAVENS. Songs of Folk & Minstrelsy. Deller and Lute.   VRS 479

THE WRAGGLE TAGGLE
GYPSIES, *and other songs.*
Deller, Lute, Recorders.   VRS 1001

*WESTERN WIND, *and other*
songs.* Deller, Guitar, Recorders.   VRS 1031 &
                                                           VSD 2014

THE CRUEL MOTHER, *and
other ballads and songs.* Deller and
the Deller Consort.   VRS 1073

VAUGHAN WILLIAMS FOLK
SONG ALBUM. *Folk arrange-
ments for 1 to 5 voices by Vaughan
Williams.* Deller and the Deller
Consort.   VRS 1055 &
                                                           VSD 2058

THE HOLLY AND THE IVY.
Medieval and later carols. Deller
and the Deller Consort.   VRS 499

*HARK YE SHEPHERDS, 20
Carols. Deller and the Deller
Consort.   VRS 1062 &
                                                           VSD 2078

CAROLS AND MOTETS FOR
THE   NATIVITY,   OF
MEDIEVAL AND TUDOR
ENGLAND. Deller and Consort
Soloists.   BG 654 &
                                                           BGS 5066

ALBUM OF BELOVED SONGS.
Deller and the Deller Consort.   SRV 141 &
                                                           SRV 141SD

CHRISTMAS CAROLS AND
MOTETS OF MEDIEVAL
EUROPE. Alfred Deller and
the Deller Consort; Musica
Antiqua of Vienna, Dr René
Clemencic, director.   BG 680 &
                                                           BGS 70680

HOMAGE TO HENRY PUR-
CELL. *24 airs and instr. works.*
Deller, Cantelo, Bevan; harpsichord, chamber ensemble. two 12″
in album, with notes.   BG 570/1

PURCELL: ODE FOR ST.
CECILIA'S DAY. Deller, Con-
sort Soloists, Chorus, Orch.   BG 559

PURCELL: ODE—WEL-
COME TO ALL THE
PLEASURES.
BLOW: ODE ON THE DEATH
OF HENRY PURCELL.
Deller, Consort Soloists, Instr.   BG 590 &
       BGS 5015

MUSIC OF PURCELL,
JENKINS AND LOCKE.
Deller, harpsichord, viols.   BG 547

*TAVERN SONGS, CATCHES
AND GLEES (including
Purcell). The Deller Consort.
            Vol. 1   BG 561
            Vol. 2   BG 602 &
                      BGS 5030

PURCELL: COME YE SONS
OF ART; BELL: ANTHEM
& MY BELOVED SPAKE.
Deller, Consort Soloists, Chorus,
Orchestra; Deller, conductor.   BG 635 &
       BGS 5047

*PURCELL: DIDO AND
AENEAS—OPERA. Thomas,
Sheppard, Watts, Tear, Bevan,
Dales; Chorus and Orchestra;
Deller, conductor.   BG 664 &
       BGS 70664

PURCELL: THE MASQUE
OF DIOCLESIAN *and Instru-
mental Music for the Play*—Deller,
Sheppard, Le Sage, Worthley,
Todd, Bevan; Chorus and
Orchestra of the Concentus
Musicus, Vienna; N. Harnon-
court, director: Deller, conductor.

BG 682 &
BGS 70682

MUSIC AT NOTRE DAME,
1200–1375. *Machaut's Notre
Dame Mass & works of Perotin.*
The Deller Consort.

BG 622 &
BGS 5045

FRENCH MEDIEVAL MUSIC,
1200–1400—*Sacred and Secular.*
Deller, Deller Consort and Consort Soloists.

BG 656 &
BGS 70656

MADRIGAL MASTERPIECES.
*Vol. 1, Jannequin, Lassus, Monte-
verdi, Marenzio, Gesualdo, Tomkins, Byrd, etc.* The Deller Consort.

BG 604 &
BGS 5031

MADRIGAL MASTERPIECES,
*Vol. 2, Monteverdi's cycle,
'Lagrime d'Amante al Sepolcro';
also Costeley, Passereau, Rore,
Arcadelt, Gesualdo, Jones.*

BG 639 &
BGS 5051

ITALIAN SONGS (16th & 17th
Centuries). *A. Scarlatti, Caccini,
Saracini, Paradisi, Wert, etc.*
Deller, lute, harpsichord.

BG 565

MONTEVERDI: IL BALLO
DELLE INGRATE (Ballet
Opera). Deller, Cantelo,
McLoughlin, Ward, soloists;
Chorus and Orchestra. BG 567

MONTEVERDI: MADRIGALI
AMOROSI (8th Book of Madri-
gals). The Deller Consort. BG 579 &
BGS 5007

DELLER'S CHOICE. *Works of
Viadona, Rore, Frescobaldi, Schütz,
Purcell, Locke, Blow, Froberger,
etc.* Deller, harpsichord, strings. BG 612 &
BGS 5038

LALANDE: DE PROFUNDIS.
Soloists, Chorus, Orchestra;
Deller, conductor. BG 640 &
BGS 5052

COUPERIN: LEGIONS DE
TENEBRES (complete). Deller,
Brown; organ, gamba. BG 613 &
BGS 5039

J. S. BACH: CANTATAS NO.
54 & 170, & AGNUS DEI.
Deller, Baroque Ensemble. BG 550

THE CONNOISSEUR'S HAN-
DEL. *Orlando's Mad Scene &
other outstanding opera & oratorio
scenes.* Deller, Brown, Poulter,
Bevan. BG 601 &
BGS 5029

HANDEL: ODE FOR THE
BIRTHDAY OF QUEEN
ANNE, & THREE CORONA-
TION ANTHEMS. Consort
Soloists, Chorus, Orchestra;
Deller, conductor. BG 661 &
70661

*HANDEL: ALEXANDER'S
FEAST. Sheppard, Worthley,
Bevan; Chorus and Orchestra;
Deller, conductor. 2 records.   BG 666 &
BGS 70666–7

MONTEVERDI: LAMENTO
D'ARIANNA and *Other Madri-
gals of Monteverdi, Jannequin,
Lassus, Marenzio, Gesualdo and
des Prez.* Alfred Deller and the
Deller Consort.   BG 671 &
BGS 70671

DUETS FOR COUNTER-
TENORS. *Canzonettas, Cantatas,
Arias, and Songs by Dering, Morley,
Jones, Schütz, Monteverdi, Blow,
Purcell, Anon.* Alfred Deller and
Mark Deller.   BG 691 &
BGS 70691

ELIZABETHAN AGE—MADRIGALS AND ART SONGS

THOMAS TALLIS: THE
LAMENTATIONS OF JERE-
MIAH & 5 HYMNS. The
Deller Consort.   BG 551

ELIZABETHAN & JACOBEAN
MUSIC. *Songs of Dowland, etc.
& instrumental pieces.* Deller,
viols, harpsichord.   BG 539

ENGLISH LUTE SONGS. Dow-
land, Morley, Campion, etc.
Deller, lute, strings.   BG 576

*MUSICAL PANORAMA OF
SHAKESPEARE'S ENG-
LAND. *Music of church, court,
streets, countryside, theatre.* Deller,
Deller Consort, recorders, viols.   BG 606

ENGLISH MADRIGAL SCHOOL, Vol. 1. *Weelkes, Bennett, etc.* The Deller Consort. BG 553

ENGLISH MADRIGAL SCHOOL, Vol. 2. *Weelkes, Wilbye, etc.* The Deller Consort. BG 554

ENGLISH MADRIGAL SCHOOL. Vol. 3. *Thomas Morley.* The Deller Consort. BG 577 & BGS 5002

ENGLISH MADRIGAL SCHOOL, Vol. 4. *John Wilbye.* The Deller Consort. BG 578

THE SILVER SWAN. *Madrigals of Gibbons, Byrd, Pilkington, Ward.* The Deller Consort. BG 624

THE CRIES OF LONDON. *Fantasies on street cries.* The Deller Consort, Ambrosian Singers, strings. BG 563

WILLIAM BYRD AND HIS AGE. *Songs, instrumental pieces.* Deller, Wenzinger viols. BG 557

MADRIGALS OF MORLEY AND WILBYE. SRV 157 & SRV 157SD

DOWLAND: 'AWAKE SWEET LOVE'. *Airs & Partsongs.* Alfred Deller and the Deller Consort: Desmond Dupré (Lute) BG 673 & BGS 70673

---

* The recordings marked thus are also issued in Great Britain by Philips/Fontana.

APPENDIX

The questions of the difference, if any, between the countertenor and the alto, and of how the mechanism of the voice-type functions, are vexed ones which have been the subject of confusing debate. Being neither countertenors nor scientists, we have felt it our duty to try to avoid adding to the mass of misconceptions; and, therefore, we count ourselves fortunate that the preparation of this book coincided with the publication (in *Music and Letters*, January 1967) of the following article by G. M. Ardran and David Wulstan. We reproduce it in full, with their kind permission and that of the journal's editor, Sir Jack Westrup, and append a brief comment by Alfred Deller.

THE ALTO OR COUNTERTENOR VOICE

By G. M. Ardran and David Wulstan

A number of attempts have been made to draw a distinction between the two words 'alto' and 'countertenor' and to imply that they refer to different voices. Recently this has been done by Frederick Hodgson (*The Musical Times*, March and April 1965) and Roland Tatnell (*The Consort*, 1965). The purpose of this article is to examine whether any such distinction is valid.

One misconception that must be brushed aside at the outset is that there is any necessary connection between part-names and voice-names, whether in Latin or in English. It is true that the names of the part-books of Barnard's *First Book of Church Music* (1641) do designate the actual voice using them, e.g. *contratenor decani primus*, but these books were kept in the stalls. In madrigalian part-books, however, which were passed round the table, or in choir-books whose parts had names such as *triplex*, *quintus* and *altus*, the intended voice is not necessarily indicated by the part-name; and, furthermore, different items in, for instance, the *altus* part of a collection may require different voices. Latin words of this type and their English equivalents are often used in theoretical and literary sources in the same way as we speak today of an 'alto' part in an organ fugue. Because of this, references to men singing the 'mean' or mean part have been taken to indicate that the mean voice was a man's voice. Charles Butler (*The Principles of Music*, 1636) and other writers of the period describe the voices quite clearly. The treble was a very high boy's voice (reaching $b\flat''$ [b flat above the treble stave]) whereas the mean was the normal boy's voice. The countertenor was the highest man's voice, and was almost always referred to by this name until the eighteenth century. It must again be stressed, however, that there is no necessary connection between a *contratenor* part and the countertenor voice, any more than there are such voices as the quint or inferior countertenor, justifiable though these epithets might seem at times.

The music of the sixteenth and early seventeenth centuries, supported by documentary sources (*see* for instance *Early English Church Music*, Vol. III, Stainer & Bell, 1964, p. viii), shows that there were as many countertenors in choirs as tenors and basses put together. This fact makes it unlikely that they were eunuchs or eunuchoid high tenors. The obvious conclusion is that they were, like their Italian counterparts, falsettists. Comparison of exposed Verse passages with Full sections or Full anthems very often reveals a striking difference between the ranges expected of the alto under these two circumstances. Whereas $e\flat$ [$e\flat$ in the bass stave] is fairly common in Full sections, $a\flat$ [a flat on the top line of the bass stave] is normally the lowest note in exposed Verse passages, except for special effects. This leads one to the conclusion that composers of the period deliberately limited solo sections to the falsetto register, expecting the 'gear change' to be used in unexposed passages. If this is so, it is certainly sound policy, since by no means all altos have an undetectable change of register.

If no historical justification can be found for distinguishing two different voices by the two terms—a conclusion that Mr Whitworth, in his article 'The Countertenor Voice' (*English Church Music*, 1965), also reaches—what is the difference between the patently falsetto 'hoot' associated with the term 'male alto' and parish sextons, and the clear tone of singers usually called countertenors, such as Alfred Deller? The fact that the two types of singer produce sounds of rather different quality cannot justify the use of two separate words unless a further range of terms, such as 'throttle-tenor' and 'bull-bass', are to be called into use to describe differences in voices other than the alto. Unless they are tenors rather than altos (in which case there is no historical or logical reason for describing them as either countertenors or altos) all altos, however named, must produce their voices by the same basic mechanism. Such refinements in tone-colour as distinguish one singer from another must be a question of natural ability and/or training in the 'placing' of the voice, that is, the control of resonance. It is clearly the larynx that must be studied in order to determine the mechanism that is common to all altos.

Slow-motion cinematography has failed to yield any incontrovertible evidence about the working of the falsetto register, and such radiography as had been done on singers was not done very systematically. The present investigations into the behaviour of the larynx were to determine what factors were common to the falsetto production of all altos, if any were indeed common, and whether a bass singing falsetto used the same mechanism as the alto, countertenor, call him what you will, using a head voice. The concept of 'registers' here will be confined to the laryngeal action, not to the resonance implied by some of the terms by which the registers are described. Head voice implies a condition of the vocal folds, not necessarily the resonance in the head; similarly with chest voice.

For the present study five male volunteers were investigated by radiography. Some were very good singers who might be described as having the 'countertenor' tone, one was a bass producing the classic 'hoot' associated with the phrase 'male alto'; the others had a tone quality mid-way between the two extremes. The neck of each volunteer was radiographed in the lateral projection. As a control this was done during quiet breathing; here they were fully relaxed, showing a wide laryngeal airway, with the vocal folds turned up into the laryngeal ventricles. Thus only a small amount of air remained in the anterior of the ventricles. These are normal appearances (*see* Ardran, Kemp and Manen, *British Journal of Radiology* [1953], *26*, 497; Ardran, Kemp and Marland, *ibid.* [1954], *26*, 201; Ardran and Emrys-Roberts, *Clinical Radiology* [1965], *16*, 369).

When the note *a* (220 cps) was sung in the 'chest' register to the vowel 'ah', all the subjects showed the appearances of a vocalized larynx, that is to say, there were prominent air-filled ventricles delineating the vocal folds over practically the whole of their length, and there was evidence of the stretching of the vocal folds by the cricothyroid muscles both from the position of the laryngeal cartilages and also from the shape of the airway. When exactly the same note was sung in the falsetto or 'head' register, all the subjects showed the same type of change: the air content of the laryngeal ventricles was reduced, indicating that a shorter length (shorter by about a quarter to a third) of vocal fold was free to vibrate. In each instance there was evidence that the cricothyroid muscles were not contracting so vigorously, and the stretching of the vocal folds was therefore less. All the subjects showed a narrowing of the laryngeal vestibule from front to back, which was associated with the backward bowing of the intralaryngeal portion of the epiglottis and its ligament. Other studies (Ardran and Wulstan, to be published) have shown that this is associated with the reduction of tension on the false vocal folds, allowing them to bulge medially. This effect can be seen on radiographs showing (i) the subject producing the note in chest voice and (ii) the same note sung in falsetto. The two sets of pictures contrast A, a subject with the so-called countertenor voice production, and B, a bass producing a hooty type of falsetto. The pictures of the production of A and B are identical.

It is suggested then, that when singing the same note falsetto as in the chest register, a shorter length only, in the middle of the vocal folds, is free to vibrate. Associated with this, there is evidence of a reduction in tension on the vocal folds. The backward bowing of the epiglottis is associated with a decrease in the distance between the body of the hyoid bone and the thyroid cartilage, and in some instances with the relative backward movement of the hyoid as well. We believe that it is this movement of the hyoid bone relative to the thyroid cartilage which is capable of moving the epiglottis and its associated tissues so that it can alter the tension on the false vocal folds, which allows them to bulge inwards and effectively damp the vocal folds; for the vocal folds cannot vibrate adequately unless associated with an air-filled laryngeal ventricle.

The vocal folds or cords are often thought of as analogous to the strings of a violin in that tightening them will raise the pitch of the note produced: the range of pitch possible by this method is limited in practice. For this reason the violin string must be stopped somewhere along its length; thus the tension remains the same but with the length effectively shortened, the pitch rises. We believe that we have demonstrated such a mechanism in the vocal cords under circumstances where an effective shortening of the cords is accompanied by a reduction in tension so that the pitch of the note produced remains the same. This is why the effect of going from chest register to falsetto is, to the singer, one of relaxation provided he is able to control his falsetto mechanism effortlessly. We have no doubt that other combinations of effective length and tension are possible, though they may be difficult to illustrate. In studies to be published, some of these matters will be deal with in greater detail in relation also to voices other than the alto. But it is clear from the above findings that the head and falsetto registers are the same, and that there is no fundamental difference between the laryngeal mechanism of one alto and another, however good or bad.

Some altos prefer not to 'change gear' at all: they prefer to extend their falsetto ranges in the Purcellian manner. Those that do change gear have to match up the registers so that the resonance of the one register will not differ markedly from the resonance of the other over the 'break'. Some singers do this unconsciously. The fact that they do so does not, however, preclude the existence of registers. Here the analogy of the 'gear change', a phrase used by almost every alto, is a good one: a car with a crash gear box almost invariably gives an audible change. Less skill is required with a syncromesh gear box unless it is faulty. Another type of singer corresponds to the automatic gear box: here changes are made without effort, but a trained listener can detect the point of change in most cases. The last type of singer has an undetectable change, like the torque-converter on rather expensive cars. But, in common with all the other types, the torque converter box works to the same end: there must be a gear change (except, of course, in the case of altos using falsetto exclusively), however gradual it may be, and no matter how involuntary.

These features are not evident in Restoration music, particularly that of Purcell; any distinction between the compasses of Full and Verse passages is indeed the reverse of that found in the early part of the sixteenth century. Whereas the chorus parts are of normal compass, the solo parts are extended either to a high or to a low *tessitura*. This suggests that the falsetto was now being cultivated for the low register and the chest voice was abandoned; this resulted in the division of countertenor voices into two specialist classes: the high and low countertenors. The most famous singer described at this period as a high countertenor was Howell, who sang, for instance, *Crown the altar* in Purcell's *Ode for Queen Mary's Birthday* in 1693. His top note was *d″* or *e″* [high *d* or *e* on the treble stave], but the parts written for him rarely descend much more than an octave below these notes. Low countertenors, on the other hand, reached as low as *e* [in the bass stave], whereas *b♭″* [*b* flat on the third line of the treble stave] was their normal top note. Purcell was almost certainly a low countertenor and probably, at the same time, a bass; this is by no means a unique occurrence and, in any case, all countertenors are able to sing bass of some sort, even if the quality differs. In church music the higher soloist sang the *cantoris* and the lower one the *decani* part. The tradition that *decani* should take the upper part is relatively modern. In the early seventeenth century, though the *cantoris* first countertenor was the principal singer, the *cantoris* second countertenor sang the same part as the *decani* first countertenor and *vice versa*; this was partly because the division in five-part antiphony could be effected in the same way as the division for five-part Full sections, and also so that neither alto part should predominate as it might when both first countertenors sang the same part against the two seconds.

The idea has been aired (in Mr Tatnell's article, for instance) that the tenor and countertenor voices were often interchangeable. This theory depends on statements in the 'Cheque Book of the Chapel Royal' such as:

> Mr. Andrew Carter . . . was sworn Gent . . . and shall come into pay [when] the next tenor or countertenor's place shall be void. (p. 14)

This surely refers to an accounting rather than a vocal manœuvre, for Carter's place was taken at his death in 1669 by Slater 'a bass from Windsor' (p. 14). This is obviously not to be construed as an indication that all men's voices were interchangeable; however, the countertenor and bass voices were, as observed before, occasionally 'doubled'.

Since there are no grounds for thinking that the sixteenth- and seventeenth-century singers who called themselves countertenors were unnatural, it follows that they must have been normal male altos singing 'falsetto' or, if preferred, 'head voice', with the option of a change into 'chest voice'. The words 'normal' and 'natural', though they can be used more legitimately physiologically, have limited value in the discussion of singing; like any other technique, singing of any kind requires no effort on the part of some, needs practice by many, and is more or less impossible to a few. 'Normal' and 'natural' must refer to all singing or none at all.

As Mr Hodgson says in his article, the word 'alto' was reintroduced later and eventually became the word by which the voice was known. At the Handel Festival of 1784 the old and new terms were used inconsistently; it cannot be inferred that they denoted different voies. In any case, the alto or countertenor was about to enter on its decline, for as Purcell and Arne had used a woman soprano in solo and chorus parts respectively, Handel and Mendelssohn were to do the same thing for the English contralto. Only in ecclesiastical surroundings did the alto survive until Alfred Deller regained a place for the voice on the concert platform.

The findings enumerated here accord with the indications that have been given by the method of ultra-slow-motion cinematography. But since this process is direct laryngoscopy with all its attendant distortions and non-stereoscopic effect, the results cannot be accepted with confidence. However, the present experiments have pointed to the mechanism involved in a gratifying way, and the day-to-day hazards that face the alto rather than the bass, such as mucus irritation (the 'grits'), which is much more annoying to the former voice than to the latter), are easily explained in view of the shorter length of vibrating vocal fold indicated by these findings, and by the fact that residues of mucus are squeezed out of the anterior end of the ventricle.

To sum up, the alto voice today is produced in basically the same way by all singers. Such differences as there are depend on good voice production as in any other voice. There can be no doubt that the classical alto produced his voice in the same way, with various modifications in the finer points of technique from period to period. Freaks undoubtedly did exist from time to time, but they cannot be regarded as the norm. The fact that Elford (mentioned by Mr Hodgson in his article) had a range as low as *a* at the bottom of the bass stave is a musicological red herring, for either Elford was a tenor, as Mr Hodgson suggests, in which case he should not have called himself a countertenor, or, more likely, this note was falsetto. It is not an impossible note to reach in this way, but to sing it in performance would make Elford very unusual. It is hoped that part of the myth of the alto-countertenor is here exploded.

Alfred Deller comments, 'This is quite the most sensible thing I have read; but, in my opinion, the view that the alto voice today is produced in basically the same way by all singers, and that such differences as there are depend on good voice production as in any other voice, is an over-simplification. It is much more complex than that, not to say mysterious. I believe that with all first-rate— certainly with great—voices, the possessor is physiologically and psychologically predisposed to the making of the actual *sound*, the timbre and quality of the voice. Of course, hard work is also necessary to acquire technique; but no amount of work will produce a clarion sound from what Nature has (inscrutably) designated a bugle.'

INDEX

Deller, Alfred—*cont.*

ings Municipal Concerts, 37, 42; and plainsong, 37; and C.C. Dramatic Society, 38; his first part in drama, 38; and the priesthood, 40; his love for Peggy, 40; Mrs Lowe comes round, 40–1; his position and prospects, 41, 44; and the Press, 42–3; early ambitions and limitations, 43, 47; marriage and honeymoon, 43, 44; and social questions and Catholicism, 44–5; and pacifism, 45, 56–7; his parents' disputes, and warfare, 45–6; *Laburnum Grove* (Priestley), 46; and the future, 47; Canterbury Cathedral choir, 48–50 *et seq.*; and other posts, 48; his range, and spirituality, 49; lack of formal qualifications, 49; Canterbury, 50–105 *passim*; and Hewlett Johnson and Crum, 52–3; his 'parts' in war-time, 55; called up, 55; a conscientious objector, 56–7, 96–7; A.R.P. or land work, 57; and the Headleys, 57–8 *et. seq.*; farm labourer at Sturry, 58–9, 68–9; and St George's Church and Group, 62; and his future, 64; and air raids, 66–7, 68–9; lives in choir school, 69; on the 'Red Dean', 70; St Augustine's College, 70; services in the crypt, 71; and *Plebs Angelica*, 72; and Purcell, 74, 94–5; and Tippett, *q.v.*, 74, 76–7, 92–6; on his voice, 76–7, 79, 168; his 'luck', 77; and B.B.C., *see* B.B.C.; a 'pioneer', 78; at Morley College, 92, 96; his true début, 93; and Purcell revival, 94–5; at Friends' Meeting House, 93, 95; at National Gallery, 96; and Church Army,

97; his 'white feathers', 97; and the peace, 98; Bergmann's advice, 100, 101; London, 100–1 *et seq.*; St Paul's Cathedral choir, 101–2, 105; Merton Park (Surrey), 103; leaves Canterbury, 104–5; his parents' last years and deaths, 106–8; his concert career expands, 108; his influence on church music, 108–9, 110; and Canon Collins, 109–10; his Christianity, 110–11; his mannerisms and habits, *see* 'Dellerisms'; and criticism, 111; and financial worries, 112; and H.M.V., 112, 160; and Dupré, *q.v.*, 112, 113, 114; and lutenists, 114–15, 116; on his interpretations, 114–17, 118–19; and 'ornamentation', 117; his mysticism, 118–20, 120; his beard, 119, 142; his melancholy, 120; and the Elizabethans, 120, 122–3; his repertoire, 122; and British folk song, 122–3; and the madrigal, 123–4; and Deller Consort, *q.v.*, 125–32; his colleagues and their difficulties, 127–30; and rehearsing, 127–8, 129; as conductor, 129 *bis*; his health, digestion and food, 130–2, 152; on hospitality, 132–3, 174; and the Duke and Duchess of Westminster, 133–4; and American hospitality, 134–5; Australia, New Zealand and Paris, 136–9; Benjamin Britten and Peter Pears, 139–40; as 'Oberon' in *A Midsummer Nights Dream*, 139–4, 145; and 'dressing-up', 140–1; an Elizabethan musical evening, 141; his beard's origin, 141; in *The Play of Daniel*, 141; no more acting, 145; on critics, 145, 174–6; on his

Deller, Alfred—*cont.*
manliness and 'a true man', 146;
on his detachment, 147–8; and
classical and modern music, 148;
and serial music, 148, 149; and
jazz, 149; and 'beat' music, 149
ter; and the Church and Christianity, 150–1; his engagements
overseas, 136–9, 152–4; his
hypochondria, 153; and 'work',
153; as a parent, 157–8; as 'man
about the house', 158; as
'adviser', 158–9; teaching and
advising, 159; and broadcasting,
159–60 (*see also* B.B.C.); and
recording, 112, 160–2, 181–90;
and Stour Music, 162–6, 171;
still in his prime as a vocalist, 166.
Interviewed: on his voice, 168;
and Bach, 168–9; on his repertoire, 169–70; on 'original' and
modern instruments, 171–2; and
ensembles, 172; on accompani-
ments, 172–3; on performance
conditions, 173–4; on hospitality,
174; on critics and musicologists,
174–6; on emotion in music,
175–6; advice to countertenors,
176–7; and to all singers, 177;
on his own life, 177–8
Deller, Mrs Beatrice (A.D.'s sister-
in-law), 45
Deller Consort, 125–32, 141, 152,
155, 156, 160, 162, 163, 165,
170, 172, 174; its reception
abroad—and in Britain, 136–7
Deller, Emma (A.D.'s sister), 3–4,
7, 8 *bis*, 13, 20, 24
Deller, Grace (A.D.'s sister), 13
Deller, Horace (A.D.'s brother),
13, 14, 20–1, 26, 51, 53
Deller, Jane (A.D.'s daughter),
112, 157
Deller, Johann Florian (eighteenth-
century composer), 11 n

Deller, Len (A.D.'s brother), 13,
20
Deller, Mark (A.D.'s elder son),
birth and childhood, 47, 48–54,
59–60, 65, 66–70, 98, 103; at
school, 103–4; in Deller Consort, 127; further details, 155–7;
his voice, 155–6; his wife, 156–7
Deller, Mary (*née* Cave, A.D.'s
mother), 3; personal details, 5,
7–10 *passim*, 12; last years and
death, 106–8; other mentions,
19–20, 23, 25, 45
Deller, Peggy (*née* Lowe, A.D.'s
wife), vii, x, 35–6; and Alfred,
38–9, 40; and A.D.'s ambitions,
43, 47; her marriage and honeymoon, 43, 44; her first pregnancy
and children, 44 n; as 'Mrs Red-
fern' in *Laburnum Grove*, 46;
her first child born, 47 (*see also*
Deller, Mark); and the future,
47; Canterbury, 48–53, 64, 69–
70; evacuated to Oxford, 53–4,
59; Lambourn (Berks), 59–60;
back to Canterbury, 64; in air
raid, 66; Sturry, 68, 69; Little
Chart and Hastings, 69; her
second child (Simon), 69; Canterbury again, 69–70; and the
peace, 98; London, 100, 103;
and Mark's entry into a choir
school, 103–4; and T. & C.
Planning Ass'n, 104 *bis*; and
Gladys Keable, 104; and A.D.'s
life work, 104, 115, 154–5; and
his beard, 141; and his 'disappointment', 143, 144; and his
tours abroad, 153, 154; and
house in Provence, 154; and the
children, 157; and the home,
158; and A.D.'s 'advice' to
others, 158–9; and Stour Music,
164–5
Deller, Rose (A.D.'s sister), 13